The Recruiter's Adventure Book!

Your Mental Map to Finding Buried Treasure in the World of Recruiting

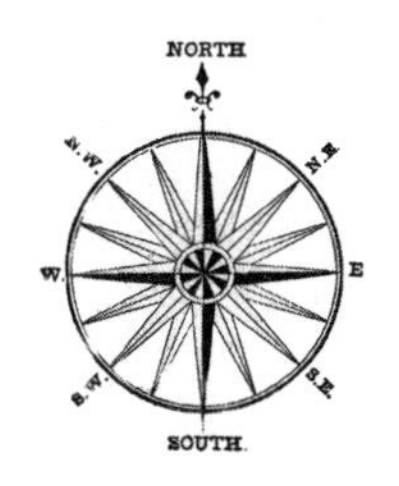

Scott T. Love, CPC

Published By
The Academy of Recruiting Mastery
7047 East Greenway Parkway
Suite 250
Scottsdale, Arizona 85254

www.recruitingmastery.com

ISBN 0-9727212-0-7

Foreword

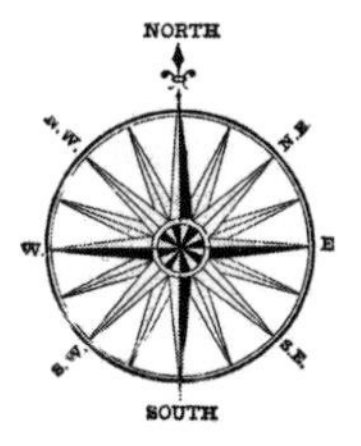

I don't care how many closes you know, or how competent you think you are with the techniques and tactics of selling; if you don't have it all together in your attitude and enthusiasm, you're wasting your time. You might as well take a ship to Mediocre Island because that's where you're sailing to without mental mastery.

True professionals know that the secret to success in selling depends more on their heart, soul, and self-confidence, than rebuttal number twenty-four. People buy from people they like. And if you don't like yourself, then you're not going to convince anyone, about anything. Well, maybe your mom. You might be able to sell something to her on pity.

Recruiting is one of the most difficult sales professions that I know of. It involves two sales at once. There is the delicate balance of finding the right fit for both employer and employee.

When I spoke at the 1997 annual convention of NAPS, the National Association of Personnel Services, I was amazed at how much expertise was needed to really be a top professional. I've never encountered any other industry where the product that you sell can come back to bite your head off. (Except for maybe the circus animal trainer.)

As a professional recruiter, to stay on the cutting edge you must keep honing your selling skills, or take a chance on being passed by someone more dedicated than you.

I'm excited for you! You made the investment in Scott's book. He's a winner and so is the information you're about to read. I'm excited about where you'll be headed in your life because of the information that follows. Scott is one of those guys who is a compulsive overachiever, but is also able to strike real harmony and balance in his life. A rare blend.

Sure, he's a big biller; and a great salesman, but I know that his real passion, his real heartfelt motivation, is to share with you the secrets of achieving mental mastery as a recruiter; to show you exactly how you can transform your mind and gain control over it to give you an edge in your industry. And this book contains his gold.

Scott's a regular ordinary guy who has stumbled on some extraordinary secrets of the industry, and had the insight to use the information to benefit himself -- and you.

Once you read this book completely, your life will be changed *if you have read it correctly.* Don't just read it. Read it and apply the simple truths to your life and to your desk. Read it and apply the simple truths to your customers both employer and employee. Read it and apply the simple truths to gain the mastery and leadership position you deserve. Read it to win.

Wishing you every sales success,

Jeffrey Gitomer

Author of The Sales Bible and

The Patterson Principles of Selling

Table of Contents

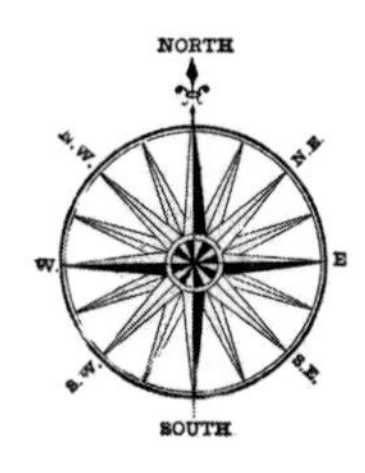

Acknowledgements

Writing a book is a team effort. Leave behind those notions in your mind of the lonely writer, isolated from the rest of the world. It is intensely creative group work. I've been blessed with a dynamic and energetic bunch of trustworthy colleagues who balance my own flaky personality with generous doses of rock-solid responsibility.

It's great having someone follow behind the wake of a creative person, someone responsible who lives in the world of reality. I couldn't have done this without the creatively competent and intensely diligent work ethic displayed by my assistant, Amanda Rembert.

And what a treat it is to have such a talented and creative writer on staff that really understands how to write and communicate on paper. Without Heather Garren, this text would be filled with sloppy choppy English, run-on sentences, and numerous tttttypos.

It's a pleasure to work with two extraordinarily talented professionals. Thanks for being patient with my lecturesque ramblings, my periods of thinking out loud too much, and my incessant whooping and hollering during deal-closing time.

To my bride: thanks for being supportive in my speaking and writing endeavors and for your friendship and companionship.

And to the eager recruiter about to embark on an exciting adventure, by all means, thank you for your business and congratulations on investing in yourself. Now get ready to see what a recruiting adventure is all about!

Chapter One

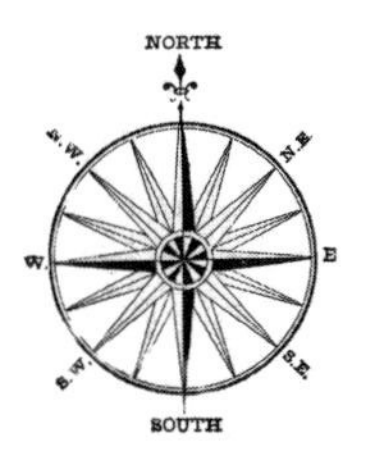

Ready Your Ship to Set Sail!

Come Aboard for an Exciting Career in Executive Search!

Ahoy, Matey! Welcome aboard, and get ready to set sail for an exciting adventure! The field of executive search and direct-hire recruiting is a career like no other. You have chosen one of the most exciting and lucrative professions offered in our society. Recruiting offers a tremendous amount of control over the level of success you reach. In this chosen profession, you will experience tremendous personal growth, unlimited financial opportunity, and a chance for...well, let's just call it character development. I can't guarantee that you'll become wealthy as a recruiter, although that's the game plan written in this book, but I can guarantee you this: you will experience every range of emotions starting on the very first day you join the industry of executive search or staffing. The range of emotions falls on the spectrum from the very high and ecstatic, sinking to the lowest of lows. One day you're flying high like a seagull in the glorious blue heavens, the next day you're a hermit crab crawling on the pit of the sea, living off the waste of decaying fish. The experience can be that drastic and dramatic. And just like any other adventure, it's filled with excitement and fun!

Who will benefit from this book:

I have specifically written this adventure book for anyone who wants to succeed: from the beginners in the industry to the big billers who can admit that they don't know it all. I don't know it all, either. I still study the basics and read the most elementary books on selling and recruiting on a regular basis, and I still learn things from them. (Even if I don't learn something new, at least I'm reminded to keep my eye on the fundamentals.) The most ideal reader is either that eager recruiter who has been in the business less than two years, or the veteran who bills less than $300,000 in annual direct-hire fees. This book will target any sort of direct-hire staffing or recruiters, including contingency recruiting, retained recruiting, and office-level staffing at the direct-hire level.

The recruiting industry provides a fabulous lifestyle and income potential. It is also one of the most difficult sales-oriented professions in the market because of the amount of variables involved. It is the only sales business where your product can actually say "No!" at the last minute. If anyone tells you that it's easy, they're either lying to you or trying to hire you. I've been recruiting since 1995. That's eight years at the date of this printing. And because I've produced consistently and have worked like a big dog all this time, it really comes out to be 56 years in dog lifetimes. And 56 years is a long time.

My billings are respectable and I'm very proud of what I've done. My direct-hire recruiting fees in recent years range from $18,500 up to $55,000, with a median fee of around $25,000 to $35,000. I've done contingency, exclusive contingency, fully engaged retained, modified contingency/retainer/engagement fee, and even owned a staffing company at one time with recruiters doing administrative level direct hire placements.

I have tried the search business almost every way imaginable. I have hired and trained and managed recruiters, while simultaneously and consistently producing from $250,000 to over $400,000 working a desk part time since the mid-90's. I have had part-time research assistants, whose primary job was to do research and candidate recruitment. But my current model is to focus exclusively on my desk, without any support staff except an administrative assistant. This model (based on my current time-intensive situation as a professional speaker and trainer) works best for my situation. It allows flexibility to spend time with my family, never having to spend more than forty hours a week in the office. In this business, once you've been around for a while and have positioned yourself prominently in your niche, you can bill significant numbers even working on a part time basis. And that's exactly the core focus of this book: **how to have an adventure in recruiting, bill out the biggest numbers that you can, and have complete fulfillment in all areas of your life.**

I spent nearly four years trying to grow a recruiting business with multiple recruiters…something that would provide a sustainable flow of revenue in spite of me being involved in it. This was a long and expensive task, resulting in an office of up to 12 employees at one time, with a high level of stress, anxiety, worry, and financial risk. What I realized was that managing recruiters wasn't something that I was particularly gifted at, nor was it something that I enjoyed as much as producing and being involved in the deal. **What I did learn to love, though, was the training component of teaching and educating my staff.** It was just the management aspect that drove me nuts. Too many moving parts for my simple brain. Nothing wrong with trying. Others have done very well with that model. At the end of the experience of trying to grow a search firm, I looked back to see that my main mistake in pursuing this was that I wasn't doing what I really, really loved.

Do what is passionate to you and your work will seem like play. Do what you love and your success is guaranteed. Focus on your key marketable assets, develop those assets, create a plan, and capitalize on them, all the while loving the process.

Perhaps you are a manager and can empathize. Perhaps you are a recruiter and are grateful you don't have your boss' job. The end result was that, after many years, hundreds of hours of effort, and tens of thousands of dollars in debt (in spite of strong personal billings the whole time), I closed up my shop, subleased my space, and went home as a solo practitioner, working out of a detached home-office. What happened once I admitted to myself what I really wanted to do was phenomenal: for the first time ever, I had the chance to really focus, like a seasoned maniacal recruiter, on my production, and within a year after making that decision I was producing at least $100,000 per quarter consistently without research assistance. And I was doing that in what really boiled down to a three or four day workweek, being able to take time to work on my speaking and training business.

I share all this with you to let you know that I can empathize with whatever situation your desk is in right now. If you've just had three counteroffers take place on the same day, I can say I've been there. If you've had your best recruiter leave your business and walk away with your

Rolodex, I've been there. If you've been frustrated with your best client who seems to have forgotten about you, I've had that happen on several occasions. And if you've thought about quitting the business...I, too, have been tempted to leave this profession, as recent as a month ago. And even now, after every deal, I still have that little voice in the back of my head saying, "Man! I'm NEVER going to close a deal that large again."

But there seems to be something about this business that just keeps bringing us back. It's addictive. It's exciting. It's like a very bad gambling habit. Just one more call might get you that star performer who will result in a $40,000 placement. You never know who will call and give you the retainer for their next Executive Vice President. And just before you emotionally give up on a search, the deal gods give you a nibble on a hot lead of some sort.

The possibilities are limitless and almost totally within your control. As a speaker in this business, I can honestly say that I love it too much to leave it. I can relate with what's going on right now in the recruiting market. My last recruiting call was this morning, not fourteen years ago. My last client rejection happened last week, not in the last decade. My ear gets sore from listening, my fingers are numb from dialing, and I go home tired and satisfied from making call after call after call…I am definitely with you. I feel the same feelings you do everyday in this business.

Once you hit a good year, you set your sights on a higher level of production. At the beginning of each month, I get excited about the possibility of what can happen. What can happen is totally dependent upon my own abilities to crank out the phone calls and close some deals, and there are no excuses. No one else is responsible for my success except for me. No one else is responsible for your success except for you. It is all up to you. And by taking the time to read another book on success, you're on the path to greatness. Winners are always willing to take the time to invest in their own success. Winners know that all they need from a book or a seminar or a tape series is one good solid idea that can help close another series of deals.

To become an expert in any field, there are four general areas that must be learned and mastered: philosophy, strategy, tactics, and habits. Learning the correct philosophy ensures that you have the right understanding of what the business is all about. The correct strategy ensures that you are headed in the right direction with a clear view of the big picture of your course of action. The tactics are the actions that you take to become successful, and the habits indicate how well you implicate the tactics. That's it. And the most important foundation, the philosophy, is the main emphasis of this book. Forget about the scripts and rebuttals and the turn-a-rounds. Throw them all out the window if people don't trust you. When you deal at the CEO level, they can usually sniff out a phony and pick up on a real winner quickly. So grow in your character, and read my other book on the systems of the search business, which focuses on the tactics and habits of the business.

It is called, The Recruiter's Compass: Tips, Tricks & Techniques for Recruiters and is available at www.recruitingmastery.com.

If you follow the formula, then you'll get the results. If you do exactly what this book tells you and master it, then you can have whatever you want to have in this business. The sky's the limit.

Stay with it and be aggressive. You were created to lead an invincible life, and the only time that you fail is when you fail to get back up and in the game. Press on, stay encouraged, and GET BACK ON THE PHONE!

Chapter Two

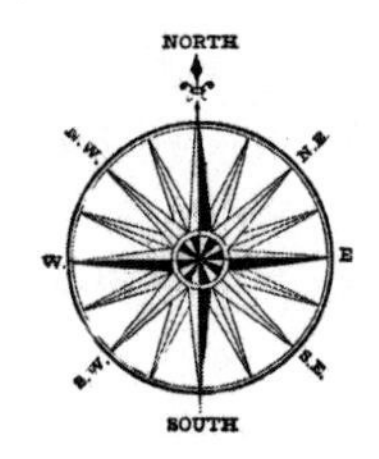

Thinking like the Captain

Developing a Heart of Greatness, Accountability, and Personal Leadership

The single greatest ingredient for success in search and recruiting is personal leadership. It is because of the way you think, your beliefs, your methodologies, and your values that people will actually follow your leadership.

Your values and thoughts serve as a lighthouse for others whom you wish to influence. Everyone is looking for leaders to follow. There is a huge void of personal leadership in the business world, and if you can provide it, people will eagerly follow.

When I was a first-year midshipman at Annapolis, I would be very surprised to hear combat veteran Marine Corps and Naval officers talk of how leadership was servanthood. I always had the impression that leadership was more the glorious task of getting a chest full of medals, but the real core of leadership is about being an unglamorous servant.

Marine Corps officers are always the last to be fed when in the field. They want to make sure the troops have enough to eat. Leadership is about putting the needs of others ahead of your needs. Serving others, as long as it is in the direction of achieving your corporate goals, is the true essence of super-effective leadership.

Leadership is about seeking out what motivates a prospective client or candidate, and figuring out how that internal motivation can be harnessed to help the team achieve its goals, thereby giving a sense of personal achievement to that employee.

The only problem with all this is that the task of having a servant's heart goes in the opposite direction of our mortal human nature. The good news about this fact, though, is that there is a simple process to real personal change on a transformational level.

If an executive or a recruiter chooses not to change and grow in this way, then his employees or others whom he wishes to influence will not consider him "followable". If he is not followable, then his prospects and teammates will only go through the motions of their tasks, leading to mediocre results or even no results at all. A real leader must be worthy of having followers, and that, more than anything, is a character issue.

Leadership is a matter of what you are, not what you do.

Many executives of today are seeking their leadership solutions in short-term, quick fix tricks and tactics. If I push this button, I'll get this response. If I just say things this way, I can manipulate my people into following me to help me reach my goals. Such shortsighted thinking can only work well on a short-term basis.

Short-term methods do not build long-term trust between leader and follower.

If longer-term change is needed, change which is permanent and is felt at the very heart of the team, then short-term fixes will not work.

Your life is a ship on an exciting adventure, and you are the captain. You ARE the Captain. You are in total control of the direction of your sailing vessel and completely responsible for the results. Many people go through life blaming others for their failure, or the economy, or the system. Maybe they didn't have the ideal family situation, maybe they didn't go to the best school, maybe their mother didn't breast feed them and offer a nurturing environment. The bottom line is that no matter what your background or your situation, the past is the past and you cannot change it.

You can change your future TODAY and design whatever sort of life you want. YOU are in control. YOU are the Captain of your ship. YOU determine where you want to sail to and what sort of adventures you want to seek out. Life is indeed an exciting adventure, and you are totally in control of your own life outcomes.

A captain of a ship is solely responsible for every event that occurs on that vessel. At Annapolis, midshipmen spend four years hearing over and over again how the captain is held completely accountable for the success or failure of the ship. If the ship runs aground while the captain is asleep, the captain is responsible. If the ship fires a missile at the wrong target, the captain is responsible. If the crew does something malicious and offensive while on liberty, the captain is responsible. The captain is completely responsible for every engineering component, every weapons system, and every sailor's action, while serving in command of that ship. It is indeed a heavy, weighty and cherished level of responsibility. And you are that captain. Your life is that vessel. You have that same level of responsibility for your own life.

The first day of the four-year Naval Academy education begins in early July every year. It is on this hot, humid, and unforgettable day that the new midshipman gives up his partying summer, his friends, and his hair in exchange for four years of a rigorous and brutal lifestyle, a nearly impossible academic schedule, extremely limited social activities, and the chance of a lifetime. Even on the first day, the starry-eyed and eager young midshipman is indoctrinated on accountability. It's one of the first things that a "plebe" learns. (The phrase "plebe", by the way, is short for plebian, an ancient Roman term classifying the bottom caste of society, just one level above dirt.) The first year is known as plebe year, where all of your God-given rights are taken away from you and given back one by one as privileges. This first-year experience gives a midshipman excellent and strong character, resulting from an artificially created environment of structured adversity. The whole point of that structured and rigidly harsh environment is to simulate the stresses and pressures of combat. It is created to help the future officer obtain a high level of self-confidence and to provide first-hand learned knowledge that there are no limits to peak performance. It helps the young teenager learn confidence and develop a mindset for expecting success, traits necessary to successfully win a war and protect our American way of life.

It is on this first day that the plebe learns his five basic responses. "Yes, sir!" "No, sir!" "Aye-aye, sir!" "I'll find out, sir!" and "No excuse, sir!"

Yes or no questions always have the "sir" at the end of them. ("Are you excited to be here, maggot?!" "Yes, sir!") Compliant responses ("Clean up your room, you filthy plebe!") always resound with an eager and enthusiastic yell of, "Aye-aye, sir!" Not knowing something is almost tolerated, as long as "I'll find out, sir!" follows the harsh inquiring question from an upper-classman. And finally, excuses for not having something done do not exist at Annapolis, and are substituted for the phrase "No excuse, sir!" ("Why didn't you clean your room, you disgusting little plebe?" "No excuse, sir!") No matter how many good excuses you have, no matter how legitimate the reason ("Sir, I overslept from studying all night and didn't have time to clean my room because if I fail this test tomorrow morning, it means I go on academic probation and can lose my weekend privileges!"), every plebe is trained to instinctively respond with "No excuse, sir!" No latitude is given for pleading, no matter how strong the case. You just sort of learn to take the hit and suck it up, developing strong character. So you just learn to take it in stride, develop a strong sense of humor, and figure it out next time.

A few months ago, I had the chance to have a conversation with a friend of mine who was the captain of a US Navy vessel. His vessel was tragically involved in an accident, which led to an international incident and a loss of human life. He was about five years ahead of me at the Naval Academy, so our experiences as midshipmen were probably similar. We studied leadership and naval science under the same professors, marched in the same uniform, and played sports on the same playing fields. We talked about the incident and how unfortunate it was that the whole thing happened. And the final conclusion he came to was that as the captain, he was completely responsible for the event. He offered up no excuse. He did not blame his crew. He did not blame a sailor for not paying attention, or a junior officer for not following proper protocol as his vessel maneuvered through the sea. He was the captain, and that's that. He was responsible. "No excuse, sir." I cannot begin to imagine the pain and agony that exist in his mind, knowing that this tragic incident happened while on his watch. In one moment, his sterling and fast track career on one of the finest and most respected vessels in the fleet ended. In an instant his life had changed forever. And at the end of the day, with heart-felt agony and a sincere sorrow for what happened, he said, "No excuse, sir". That level of courage, to take the hit, is indeed rare and requires vast levels of heart and character.

While our lives as recruiters will probably never reach the same level of responsibility that my friend held on his vessel, we are still accountable and responsible for our desks, for our production, and for our commitment to our clients and managers. As captain of your life you cannot offer up excuses when something goes wrong. It does not matter to the client who has been neglected that your computer lost all of your information, or that your secretary forgot to send their message. The outcome is the same to them. In taking control of your own life, you must grab hold of the courage needed to say, "No excuse, sir". You must accept responsibility when doing so is detrimental to your personal interest. This is how you make the life transformation from "plebe" to "captain". "No excuse, sir!"

No matter what your situation in life or where you are in your professional career, there are three beginning steps to growing in character and developing a heart that is worthy of greatness. It doesn't matter whether you are an executive, a secretary, a production manager, a sales representative, an engineer, a schoolteacher, or a homemaker. Everyone is a leader. Everyone influences others and is influenced by them. And in the business of executive search, you are indeed a leader to your clients, your candidates, and every single person that you talk to. Part of success in the field of staffing is setting yourself apart from your competitors. If you can build up a "following" of those who you contact regularly, then YOU will be the one who gets the call when there is a search need or when someone is ready to make a move. If you develop a heart of greatness and develop within yourself the mind of a leader, then people shall eagerly follow you.

If you are even a first-year rookie starting at the bottom of the organization, you must still assume the heart of a leader and grow in that area. As you do, if you are faithful in those little items of team leadership, you will be rewarded and given greater levels of responsibility. People want to be influenced. People want to follow someone who is followable. A good recruiter can develop those character qualities. When you have those qualities, people seem to be able to sense it over the phone.

The first step of growing in leadership is to (I) **have a prosperous heart.** A prosperous heart believes that there is room in the organization for everyone to achieve satisfaction and for every candidate and client to grow in prosperity. Everyone can achieve the victory when the team does, and the team does not achieve victory until everyone does. By ensuring that every single person in the organization wins when the company wins, you increase the probability of the team achieving its goals. A prosperous heart does not hold the glory for itself. Rather, at the end of the day, the leader with the prosperous heart appears invisible to the team. A successful leader will have his team members carrying on about how they accomplished the tasks themselves.

Remember that a good recruiter never has to say "thank you". If you walk the walk and produce results, your clients will be elated with the awesome superstar that you just placed in their company. They'll get excited about sending you the fee. The candidate will be grateful as well. If you have this philosophy, develop a solid strategy, implement sound tactics, and develop good habits, you will never have to worry about a recession. You might not make as much as in a good and strong market, but you will always be closing deals.

The second step of growing in leadership is to actually (2) **live in a way that is congruent with your heart.** This means that you need to clearly identify those values and principles that guide the way you do business and live your life. Once you have identified those, you can develop a certain sort of code. In the boy scouts, they call it the Scout Oath.

"On my Honor…

…I will do my best…

…To do my duty to God…

…and my country…

…and to obey Scout Law;…

…To help other people at all times…

…To keep myself physically strong…

. . . mentally awake. . .

. . . and morally straight."

And even the Scout Law is taught to boys at an early age, guiding them in principles and values that follow them the rest of their lives.

"A Scout is

Trustworthy

Loyal

Helpful

Friendly

Courteous

Kind

Obedient

Cheerful

Thrifty

Brave

Clean, and

Reverent."

Who wouldn't want their child to learn these things? You can imagine that this is the type of person that you yourself would want to do business with. The guiding force of any success, whether in business or home life or community involvement, is based on values and character. It's all about personal leadership.

In the military they have a code of conduct. For physicians, it's the Hippocratic Oath. Many professions have some sort of oath or ceremony to dedicate their newly indoctrinated members into a commitment toward a higher calling. Once that calling has been identified, you can start making clear decisions within the framework of that calling or code. It is that calling or code that keeps our focus on what is the right thing to do when temptations abound. At the Naval Academy, I learned about making the "hard right", a concept that seems to provide a foundation for living and decision-making in the military profession. That "hard right" decision is the decision that a military officer must make, even though it is unpopular, goes against pragmatic expedience, or is not in the career interest of the officer. It is the decision to stick to the code of honor and not jeopardize that moral commitment. At the Academy, we would actually go through scenarios that we would face in the fleet. This four-year intensive training would give us a foundation for decision-making.

Have you ever written down your values? What really guides you through the day? Here's an exercise. Tonight before you go to bed, I'd like for you to journal about these things. Write them down. If you don't know, just start writing and it'll come to you:

Assuming you had won the lottery and had fulfilling relationships in your life, what would motivate you?

What would get you excited each day?

What do you value? Do you value time? Family? Love? Prosperity? Honor? Influence? Persuasion? Excellence? Effectiveness? Jot down a few immediate notes below:

____

____

____

____

____

____

Once you have identified these values and clarified them, commit them to memory. What are the three or four singular values that guide your life?

1)

____

____

____

2)

____

____

____

3)

____

____

____

4)

____

____

____

Easy to do, yet difficult to do as well.

Based on the values you expressed above, develop your Personal Mission Statement. Yeah, yeah, we've been through this before at our last company retreat, you're saying. Sure, Scott. We did this two years ago when our search firm went off to some conference center in the pines and had some Granola-eating new age consultant with a ponytail and diamond earring guide us through a mission statement according to ancient aboriginal tradition. And after the incense cleared and the drums stopped beating, we sat there scratching our heads asking ourselves how we could make a buck off of this mission statement. So we blew it off and went to the phone and started cold calling again.

I can understand and appreciate the recruiter's tendency to avoid the cerebral and focus on the phone. Got it. Know it. Kind of agree with this reluctance to focus on the analytical side of things. Yet remember that no matter how many phone calls you make in a day, if you do not come across as one who is congruent, you'll never hit the next level of your career.

If you ever ask what guides a CEO of a successful company, he'll tell you it's his values. It's not his profits or his commitment to the shareholders. That might be a tangible objective for him, but successful people know that the secret to success is to follow a higher calling; to live a life that is worthy and noble and makes a big impact in the world. It's more than just another telephone call. It's about making the biggest impact that you can to the guy or lady on the other end of the line. If you develop clarity of purpose in your life, it comes across on the phone. If you want to grow in your confidence, develop a character that is worthy of being confident in. If you want to do business at the CEO level, start thinking like a CEO.

The third step of growing in leadership is to (3) **communicate this trust to those around you.** Because you are living in a predictable sort of way in alignment with your heart or code of values, others around you will see this commitment. If you are in a supervisory position, you need to articulate the values of your group in some sort of fashion. If you are dealing with clients and candidates, integrate your Core Values and Purpose into your sales presentations and recruiting calls.

Marketing is all about being different. And if you articulate your belief system to a prospective candidate or client, you'll be different. By telling them what motivates you as a recruiter, they'll believe that you don't see candidates as walking invoices. They know that you have a mission and a purpose in your career and will be able to tell a difference in your enthusiasm. Enthusiasm sells. Congruent enthusiasm wins clients for life and creates a fan club.

By communicating the spirit of these beliefs to your team, you are creating silent accountability. People who believe in your team will actually start following your very own commitment to those same values and principles. By having a unified team whose heart is beating in the same way, trust begins to develop. This trust is a byproduct of the personal transformation that you develop. Leadership is a very personal issue, and cannot be institutionalized. The true measure of success as a leader is based on the amount of trust and commitment that he or she earns from his fellow teammates, clients, and candidates.

Many new leaders will be surprised at how easy the tactical elements of leadership really are. That's because leadership is more of an issue of character than of competence. It is still an issue of competence, but more of the key measurements of leadership are focused on character-related issues. By taking these first three steps to developing a heart for leadership, you will have others around you take notice and become influenced by you, and begin to see you authentically in your role as a master of influence.

Chapter Three

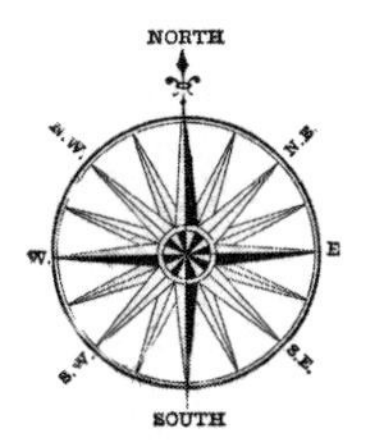

Celestial Navigation

Guiding Your Mind to Success

One of the most interesting and fascinating concepts I learned at Annapolis was the concept of using the stars to guide you. The ancient mariners obviously didn't have GPS or other electronic navigation gadgets to guide them. They had to use two concepts in sailing that still apply today: celestial navigation, and dead reckoning.

Dead reckoning is the concept of using your past course to determine where you are going to be in the future. You simply look at where you've been, assume that you're going the same speed in the same direction, and you can sort of predict where you will be at a certain time. Not perfect, but it gives you a good idea of where you're headed. Celestial navigation isn't perfect either, but it was extremely effective in giving ancient mariners a general idea of where they were. Imagine this: It's the middle of the eighteenth century, and you're sailing on a vessel from England to the colonies. The ship has no motor, no engine, and no electronic navigation equipment. But it has a compass and it has a sextant, and that's all it needs (along with nautical charts) to determine where it is headed.

The sextant is a tool used to measure angles of a star relative to your position on the ship, as well as between the star and the surface of the earth. Through various mathematical concepts and formulas, the sextant makes reference of those unchanging, predictable, and comfortably bright celestial beings gracefully lingering over the dark black evening sea. How comforting it must have been for the ancient and seasoned mariner to find his way across that vast ocean in the cold blinding darkness of night.

Because of historical nautical records, sailors would be able to predict exactly the azimuth angles of various stars, the moon, and the planets; all following the calendar year. Because these records would predict the movement of the celestial bodies, the sailor would be able to factor that, in relation to the curvature of the earth, and have a general idea of where the ship would be during its voyage.

This truly fascinated me during my third year at Annapolis. We spent a good part of an entire semester learning an ancient nautical craft, which we'd never use again. Never again since that class did I have to find my way across the ocean using the stars. Instead the position would be plotted on the chart based on GPS and other navigational tools. But at least it was fun to learn.

In your voyage as a recruiter, keep following those values and principles that are always constant, always there, and always guiding you on your path. And know that God gave you your own powerful tool: the ability to harness energy that you might not even know exists within you. The sextant, the compass, and the nautical chart: all these are excellent tools, but unless applied properly, they are worthless. And the most powerful tool that your Creator has blessed you with is your gray, ugly brain. Yes, the brain is certainly one of the most ugly parts of the human body. Come on. Let's not kid ourselves. At least we don't have to look at it all day.

Mental achievement is the single greatest principle that keeps a big billing recruiter on the phone. Mental toughness, mental mastery, mental achievement: all these terms refer to the recruiter learning the art of harnessing all that power of your tiny little gray matter, and using it to explode your production.

Your mind cannot determine the difference between fiction and reality. Consider a nightmare that you have when you're sleeping. You wake up in the middle of the night dreaming that Freddie Kruger has been chasing you, and you're overwhelmed by fear and emotion, so much so that your physiology has been affected. Your heart is beating at a high rate of speed, your breathing is faster, and you are sweating. The physical state of your body responded to an imaginary influence from your brain. The reality is that Freddie Kruger doesn't exist but that your body believed that it did and responded accordingly.

I remember as a child how, when seeing a scary scene in a movie, my parents would tell me, "Scotty, it's okay. It's all pretend. Those people are actors pretending to do those things."

Logically, I do indeed understand this concept. But I also saw Jurassic Park and I nearly wet my pants. You and I know that dinosaurs don't exist in modern times. But I still can't stand even thinking about certain parts of that movie. (Except for the lawyer scene. I think I even heard some clapping in the back of the theatre when the lawyer was eaten.)

Take that same mental focus, and apply it to seeing yourself producing whatever figure you want to produce. If you don't really think you can do it, then pretend that you can do it. Start asking yourself how a big-billing producer makes a phone call, and emulate that. Visualize yourself responding to the way you produce at that level. Visualize yourself just wrapping up your deal putting you over your mark, and use that as leverage in influencing others. Sit the way a big biller sits. Talk the way a big biller talks. Stand up and change your physiology the way a big biller stands. Walk the way they walk; use your hand gestures the way they use theirs.

My father was a career Marine Corps officer when I was a lad. I lived in Hawaii, Japan, Quantico, Virginia, Camp LeJeune, North Carolina, and Camp Pendleton, California. I had always wanted to be a pilot when I grew up, so I found the best undergraduate school for the naval service, and was able to get an appointment. That's no small feat. You first must receive a nomination from your Senator or Congressman, and then must compete with over 10,000 applicants for only 1,500 positions. And even if you make it in, nearly a third of your class quits or gets kicked out for academic reasons or for violating the honor concept. I spent my entire youth, since the sixth grade, focusing on this vision. I thought about being a pilot everyday in high school. My freshman, sophomore, and junior years at the Academy were dedicated to the exciting career of jet aviation. And then my senior year, just a few months before graduation and the time when seniors choose their respective branch of naval service, I found out that I was N.P.Q., Non Physically

Qualified. The migraines that I had been having would keep me from achieving a boyhood dream. All because of a stupid headache. This was very disappointing, but the ensuing events had an extremely positive impact on me. The migraines became worse, and I was sometimes physically unable to do my job as an officer effectively, so I was going to be discharged for medical reasons from the naval service. I was placed on shore duty and spent countless hours in doctor's offices trying out new medicines, which had bad side effects.

After a few months with no relief, I was instructed to begin visiting the psychiatry section of the hospital for experimental techniques in migraine relief. Okay, thanks, I thought. Thanks for making me feel like a freak. I even remember seeing the 'nutso' section of Portsmouth Naval Hospital in Portsmouth, Virginia. (This was also the new home of a sailor who tried to kill me a few years prior. Yes, a sailor was stalking me and waiting for me to board the ship when he was going to shoot me while he was standing watch with a very loaded Colt 45 pistol. Luckily, or should I say by divine intervention, I was transferred to a two-day school at the last minute, giving him enough time to reason with his sane side and turn himself in. But that's another sea story…)

The doctors at the psychiatric unit told me they believed that if I was to raise the body temperature in my fingers and toes, it would draw the blood away from my head, giving me relief from the migraine. I would do this through progressive relaxation and biofeedback.

Progressive relaxation is a way that you begin relaxing each part of the body through certain mental techniques and breathing. With biofeedback, I would cause the temperature of my fingers and toes to increase. The temperature of your skin is at room temperature, usually around 73 degrees. They would hook me up to a machine that would monitor the temperature of my skin on my fingers and my toes and was represented in graph form on the screen of a computer.

In a matter of weeks, I learned to increase my body's exterior skin temperature by about 15 degrees in 15 minutes! I would visualize placing my hands and feet slowly into a hot bucket of water. This mental imagery would translate into a physiological change in my body.

Your mind cannot determine the difference between reality and fiction, and your body will respond accordingly. I could literally see the chart of my body temperature rise on the screen of the computer, as if someone was moving the knobs of an "Etch-a-Sketch".

This lesson changed my life. I was intrigued by this mental power and began reading books on mental toughness and positive thinking. I learned that you attract into your life whatever you want simply by focusing on it. If you expect good results, then you get good results. If you anticipate failure, then you get failure. The power of your mind is probably your single greatest ally or enemy, depending on what you think about and what you focus on. This is not some sort of new age mysticism; it is biological, and it is the single greatest reason why people become successful.

If deep down inside you really do not think you can become a big biller, then you have a choice. This business is not for everyone. You either love it or you hate it. I think I mentally quit every week for my first two months when I started. But I learned to love it because the success that you have in this business is a direct result of your improvement as a person. If you become a better person, then you make more money. What a deal!

If you choose to work your way through this doubt, then I congratulate you! The choice to win is the most important first step. You must choose to be successful, whether it's in this business or anything else. You must decide. You must say to yourself, "I will do whatever it takes to be an achiever." Whether it's as a farmer, a doctor, a salesperson, or a counselor, you must decide to win. Success is a conscious choice. People do not accidentally become successful. Success leaves clues, and if you study people who are successful, you will find common areas in their lives that lead to their successes.

Here's a nine-step action plan for you to develop mental achievement:

- ❑ **Step One**: Decide that you will be able to jump over this most important hurdle.

- **Step Two:** Visualize yourself as a big biller. You must mentally "act as if" you are a big biller.

- **Step Three:** Change your physiology. Sit the way a big biller sits. Stand the way a big biller stands. Laugh the way a big biller laughs.

- **Step Four:** Create an action plan to achievement. Simply write down when you will be able to produce the number that you want to hit. What are the steps that you need to take to hit this number?

- **Step Five:** Write a letter to yourself. Write a letter and date it December 31st of the year in which you hit your goal. Write the letter to yourself to who you are today. Let yourself know what the future is like at that point. Tell yourself about your lifestyle. Tell yourself the emotions you felt when you hit this important goal. How did you feel when you closed the deal that put you over your goal? What emotions did you experience? What challenges did you have to overcome? What is your lifestyle like at that income level? What sort of house do you live in? What does the leather in your car smell like? Imagine driving home in your car to your house at that point and experience the full emotions of that achievement. Your mind cannot distinguish between fiction and reality, and by doing this; you are creating the expectation for success.

- **Step Six:** Read every day. Set up a reading program. Invest in your own personal achievement library. Read for at least fifteen minutes on a book pertaining to success, achievement, sales, personal effectiveness, personal development, or motivation. You are in control of your career, and it is up to you to take action on this. No one else will know whether you are doing this except for yourself. (See the Appendix for a recommended reading list. Visit my website, www.recruitingmastery.com, for a frequently updated view of this list, absolutely free.)

- **Step Seven:** Watch training tapes and listen to audiocassette tapes. I've personally invested thousands of dollars in audio and videotapes. I have over two hundred cassette tapes and over sixty hours of video training. Many of these tapes are those that I purchased before I started producing respectable numbers. When I heard of a big biller who produced more than me, I would fly out to meet him and see his seminar, and purchase every audio and videotape that I could get my hands on. I'm a nut about that, I suppose. I'm a freak about education. You should be an education freak as well. Tommy Hopkins says that you can always tell how successful the top producers are by how they continue to learn once they know it all. It's up to you to do the research on the different products that are available, and I've bought pretty much every product for our industry. All of them have some value to add. Some are for beginners, some for more advanced and skilled veterans in the business. But start your library right now.

- ❑ **Step Eight:** Here's a gut check. Are you ready for success? Are you willing to do what it takes to succeed in the recruiting industry? If not, then put the book down because you're wasting your time. If you are, then turn the page and get ready to make a commitment to yourself.

I promise to myself

that I will follow the above eight steps,

on a regular and daily basis,

continually striving to reach higher and higher.

Signature: ______________________________

Date: ______________

- ❑ **Step Nine:** Good job, hero. Now find a buddy or a manager to keep you accountable. Yeah, that's right. Put down the book, call a friend or manager, and tell him or her what you're going to do. Ask your friend to keep you accountable. I guarantee you that if you don't find someone to hold you accountable, then your odds significantly decrease that you will follow this system. It is very rare for someone to be able to muster up the self-discipline that it takes to do everything in this system. It is also very lonely and this business sure can be a disappointment from time to time, so find someone to keep you accountable.

Chapter Four

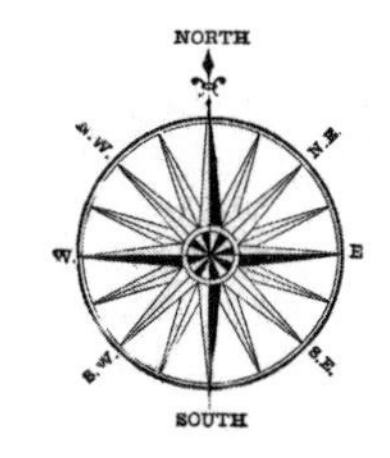

Serendipity

The Art of Expectation

Recently I read an article in the Wall Street Journal that described the trends in the high technology marketplace. The article mentioned how in every recession, the technology innovations, which were unforeseen immediately prior to the recession, gained enough momentum to bail out the whole technology sector. The innovations included everything from the PC market, the software operating systems market, and the Netscape innovations that allowed graphics to be transmitted over the Internet. In each of these scenarios, it was somewhat serendipitous that the "cure" for that particular recession was revealed. This phenomenon seems to unequivocally be a predictable element of tech recoveries, and the article went on to say that many economic experts are expecting such an event to break the economic slow-down of the first half of the 2000's decade. In a sense, it is a level of "expectant serendipity".

When my wife and I moved back to Asheville, North Carolina, after living in the Phoenix area for about seven years, we were renting a nice apartment in a rather rural area complete with winding mountain roads nearby. Perfect roads for a jog. Not too steep, with enough hills and curves to make it interesting. But the only bad thing about the road next to the apartment was that it went by a small and old-looking mobile home park. Now, I don't have anything against mobile home parks. I've seen my fair share of them, even up close. But trailer parks always seem to have some sort of unpredictable sense about them. I don't know, maybe I've watched too many episodes of "Cops!" but every time I ran by this particular trailer park, I always got a sense of what I'd call "Negative Serendipity". I have no idea if Negative Serendipity exists, but I'll go ahead and coin that phrase, right here and now. I'll define Negative Serendipity as the event that occurs when people expect something really, really bad to happen to them.

One day I felt the Negative Serendipity was particularly strong as I jogged past the trailer park, even though nothing had happened. Not a thing. I didn't see or hear any Trans Am's speeding by me with failing mufflers. I heard not a single baby cry nor the phrase of, "Take that diaper off your head and put it back on your sister!" coming out of the park. "That's odd," I thought. I at least expected a band of dogs to come out of there and start chasing me.

On the way back, I was expecting to see some sort of scary, foamy-mouthed, smelly dog to come bolting out of the trailer park to chase me and bite up my new shiny running shoes. Sure enough, as I approached the entrance, a pit bull comes trotting out on a mission. And that mission was me.

I paused, grabbed a rather large rock, which was subsequently replaced by a rather large heavy stick, and slowed my pace to a standstill. I waited. The dog sniffed. I held my breath. The dog sniffed again. I stood still, very still. Knowing full well that a chasing movement ignites the irresistible canine instinct to attack prey, I stood as still as a pigeon-pooped statue. The dog left the mobile home park, but not in my direction. He turned in the direction that I needed to go to get away from the park and back to my apartment. So I had to run TOWARDS the smelly dog that was waiting to eat me.

I felt confident with my weapon, which was actually a cheap gray signpost from a blown-away garage sale sign. I held the imaginary sword firmly in my hand, trying to avoid splinters, and began to feign confidence as I approached

Smelly Dog. "Get away from me, Smelly Dog! Go home, Smelly Dog!" I thought to myself.

Smelly Dog ran into the bushes, probably on his way to chase after some other unsuspecting transplanted suburban jogger. When I came home and told my wife of my adventure, she said, "Scott, you always seem to have experiences with dogs chasing you when you're jogging or biking." True, I thought. She's absolutely right. I do seem to expect dogs to chase me. "But I'm just preparing for the worst," I responded, defending my position.

I thought about it, and as it turns out, every time I've ever anticipated or expected a dog to chase me on a run or a bike, it has always happened.

Perhaps it's just my choice of neighborhoods. But I think that whole experience is sort of an example of how people attract bad things to them. So many people continue to expect others to reject them; to connive and plot against them. They assume and expect a certain event to materialize and reoccur in their lives, and that's exactly what happens.

Expect a smelly pit bull to come chasing you out of a trailer park, and that's probably what will happen.

Asheville seems to be teeming with artists. It is a lovely eclectic mountain town in Western North Carolina, which seems to be a haven for artists. There are artists on every corner, almost literally. I interviewed an artist to do some graphic design for my company. She showed me some of the things she had done with photography, and I was moved and impressed. She would take existing photographs, scan them in to her computer, and do some impressive graphic design, creating a long lasting and colorful, original memento of a loved one. She mentioned that she just wished that she could make more money by selling her art. I told her that sometimes I would coach people to help them explore their uniqueness, creating a strong brand and helping them to capitalize on their abilities. She took me up on the offer. We worked out a bartering arrangement, where she would take some photos of my little boy and, through her graphic design abilities, create some unique and lovely art. In exchange, I would give her a one-hour coaching session.

We met a few weeks later, and I was so excited about what she had done to the photos of my little boy! She created this beautiful arrangement of my son's snapshots and gave my wife and me a memento that we would forever cherish. She was talented, more so than your typical artist. She possessed a very rare ability and her art was emotionally moving.

I met with this artist for our coaching session and the first thing I started to do was to just ask her questions; questions about her values, her purpose as an artist, and her motivations. We progressed through our session and came upon the idea of her creating a niche targeted towards children's photography. She would take existing photos of children and create a colorful collage, which parents would love to pay handsomely for. I explained to her that the first rule of branding is identifying what is unique about you. Once you do this, your whole image and persona and gifts are focused on this brand. Branding today is similar to the ways cattle are branded on ranches. Your brand identifies you. It is a clear indication of who you are, where you are from and what is unique about you. So we focused on her uniqueness and her talents and her values and how we could turn her gift into cash flow. We came up with several ideas related to her craft...but one idea stood out. "Betty, why don't you just call the CEO of Olan Mills, a national photography chain? Tell him that you have a graphic design concept that you can sell to them, as a consultant, where they can take their existing photographs, their existing client base, and their existing marketing relationships, and turn all of their existing inventory in to another source of impacting revenue, all with minimal cash outlay." The idea would have to work, I thought. I was so excited about the climatic event of our coaching session and this "aha!" result that would catapult her to riches and fame in the art world. I sat back in my chair, smiling smugly inside about my breakthrough idea, excited about her ensuing fortune. She said, "Scott, I don't think I could call anybody like that. Only bad things happen to me. I'm tired of being poor, but I guess I'll never get out of being poor. I just can't see myself doing anything like that."

No, no, no! I thought to myself. Don't quit! I sighed, and said, "Betty, what's the worst thing that could happen? They could say no, but then you go on to the next prospect." I tried to breathe life into her tired old soul, but the fire just wasn't lighting. It was a futile attempt to help someone that couldn't be helped. Sadly, she had conditioned herself to expecting a life of not winning; a life of taking whatever comes your way, a life of depressing and unfortunate mediocrity. Her dreams would never be realized because the drive to try just wasn't there. The negative serendipity just took over. She expected to fail and didn't want to try.

I think what my artist friend faced was probably one of the more difficult challenges that we as recruiters face. It's the ongoing saga of the human story, just like that educational movie that we all saw in the fourth grade about the amoeba and the electric shock. The scientists in the movie would send an electric shock to an amoeba and at the same time display a bright flash of light. The amoeba would react by recoiling into a safer position, then relax and uncoil into its shape at rest. They would shock the amoeba again, flashing the light simultaneously, and the amoeba would recoil again. Over and over they did this to the poor suffering amoeba. Finally, the scientists would just flash the harmless bright light with no shock. The amoeba would recoil again, expecting to feel the pain of the electric shock. Bright light, no shock, immediate recoiling reaction. The amoeba had become conditioned to the pain associated with the shock, even though the shock wasn't present. The expectation was there based on previous experiences.

Most rookie recruiters experience a fair amount of shock with rejection on the telephone. It hurts to be rejected, even if there is no physical pain associated with the experience.

As children we grow up with rejection all around us. From the things that our parents say to us, being totally human and imperfect, to the teasing and incessant cruelty that young children can display. It's tough being a kid, and that's exactly where our formative beliefs are shaped. Our whole perception of ourselves and where we fit in the world is shaped at an early age, and we bring all of that with us to work everyday in the recruiting world, schlepping the invisible baggage, plopping it on our desk each morning as we make our entrance in to the office.

"Good morning, Bob. Nice baggage you got there."

"Thanks, Joe. Say, I really admire how you carry around your self-defeat each day to work."

"No kidding? Thanks for noticing, Bob. And that inferiority complex is quite stunning, I must admit!"

"Well, that's because my mother didn't breastfeed me. And being picked last on the kickball team in second grade sure has a way of affecting my candidate recruiting calls."

Everybody has it. But nobody will admit it. It is what makes the whole human experience so frustrating and exciting and adventurous. When negative things happen, people expect them to continue happening, leading to disappointment, frustration, and jaded cynicism. It is easier to become cynical because then you cannot get hurt. Whenever you make a sales call or a recruit call, you are putting yourself on the line. You are telling the other person, "Hey, I'm making myself vulnerable here, asking you if you're open to looking at other things." And if they say no, then the rejection feelings can sink in. But for now, realize that you just have to get over the feelings of negative expectation. Instead, no matter how many times people tell you no, expect a yes.

I challenge you to think with positive expectancy for thirty days. I challenge you to get out of bed each day and say, "Today is going to be the most exciting day of my life!" Tell yourself that on your way to work. Okay, it might sound hokey and homespun, but give it a try. You don't have to do this in front of anyone, and I'm okay if you never tell anyone that you really do this, tough guy. Yeah, you're so tough. And if you're cynical, try it anyway and tell me it doesn't work and that you were right and that I'm full of crap. But try it for thirty days. Expect the clients to want to retain or hire you. Expect the candidates to eagerly explore your opportunities. By taking this thirty-day challenge, you'll be surprised at how many truly serendipitous things seem to find you! Just don't expect pit bulls to come chasing you out of trailer parks.

Chapter Five

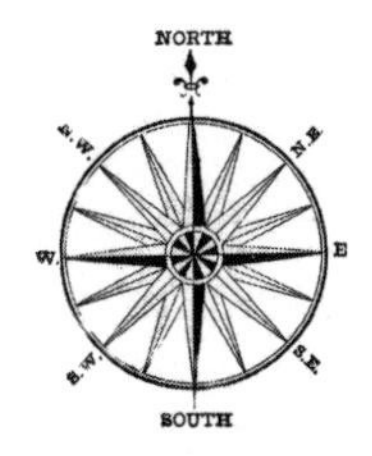

Toss Your Baggage Overboard

Regain Control of Your Attitude

There are five steps to overcoming this emotional baggage that weighs you down, to re-gain positive control over your attitude and to keep those previous negative experiences from causing us to recoil in pain whenever someone simply turns the light on. This is your first step to finding the buried treasure in the world of recruiting: admit that you have room to grow, and identify those specific areas of improvement. Write down your strengths, as well as your areas of improvement. Take a "personal achievement inventory" about you:

Step One: Personal Achievement Inventory

1. What are my greatest strengths? What is unique about me?
2. What is my greatest weakness?
3. What are my positive reinforcing beliefs about me?
4. What are my negative beliefs about me? What are those anchors that are keeping me from sailing to an adventurous world?

Step Two: Let your mind run wild.

No, this isn't a racy romance novel, although that might be fun to write one someday. Ask yourself this question: What would happen if I achieved every goal that I set? If I didn't have these anchors in my life, those weighty beliefs that hold me down, what would be the possibilities of my adventures? What would I achieve in my life if I knew that I could not fail?

By doing this, you are creating a new Life Achievement Baseline™. This is the baseline that you will establish to begin thinking about yourself and your potential from now on. Instead of the limited thinking and the anchors holding you down, you are now allowing yourself, giving yourself permission, to unleash your full potential and set sail. There are no limits. There are no barriers. There is only you and the open ocean waiting for you to begin experiencing your true destiny.

One of the best exercises that you can develop is a mental exercise of Positive Forward Meditation™. By using the technique of Positive Forward Meditation, you can actually harness the power of your mind to create positive serendipity in your life. You can daydream your problems being solved and your future being realized right in front you. Create a time every week when you can just sit quietly and review your yearly and monthly goals. Visualize yourself reaching those goals. Do not just see yourself reaching them. Experience them. Sit quietly where you cannot be disturbed, at a time when you do not have the normal pressures of the week. For myself it's every Sunday morning. I'll usually sit at my favorite spot in the house, have my journal in front of me, and start writing. I'll write about where I want to go in my life.

Free your mind. Imagine yourself achieving wild success, both at your desk and in life. Don't have any limits; just be creative.

Step Three: Lay in Your Course

When I was a young officer, I was third in command of a U. S. Navy minesweeper. It was the USS Fortify. It was a wooden ship without a lot of metal on it because the magnetic signature given off by ships is one of the ways that mines are activated. Mines are cheap and effective and can give the enemy a strong strategic advantage. They're also difficult to find and dangerous to detonate.

The minesweepers have a difficult and unglamorous job of hunting for and sweeping live mines during combat situations. They are usually the first ship to lead the fleet into a new harbor. Imagine Iraqi troops firing on you as you sweep the harbor of mines so that amphibious landing craft can safely place Marines on the beach. Either contact with a ship, pressure from a ship, or the magnetic signature given off from a ship's hull activates mines.

The ship I was on was made sometime prior to the Korean War, and I was her Operations Officer during the time of the Gulf War. I was 22 years old, third in command, and clueless. I had no idea what the hell I was doing on that ship. I just learned to act like I knew what I was doing, to listen to my senior officers and senior enlisted, and to fake it. I faked the confidence that I had and gradually became more confident in my role as I learned what the whole minesweeping deal was all about. I grew up quickly in the two years that I was on that little wooden boat, and developed strong management and leadership skills. Leading recruiters is one thing. Leading a bunch of raucous eighteen year olds who hate both you and the Navy is another thing. But it was one of the best experiences of my life, especially when we got underway to do minesweeping exercises.

We were a small ship, 173 feet long, and had a crew complement of anywhere from forty to sixty sailors on board. We were the smallest ship in the fleet, and at the time of a minesweeping operation we were the most important. Because we didn't have large fuel tanks we couldn't get underway for more than a few days. So we would usually get underway at 7:30AM everyday, returning around 6:00 that night. We would usually steam around the green waters close to the Norfolk and Little Creek harbors in Virginia. Sometimes we would make trips down to Charleston before they closed the Navy base there.

There was never a day when we did not know where we were going. Everyday we had a plan for where we were sailing. Sometime the plan would change, but each day we would lay in a course for where we were headed.

Look at where you want to be in the next five years. At this point, think only in terms of billings, because that should be your primary focus on your goals. Let's just be realistic. You spend more hours at work than at home, so you should spend more time thinking of and planning for your production. Don't worry about tomorrow or next month. We'll discuss in the next chapter how you specifically set up an action plan to reach your goals.

When you think about the production levels that you wish to hit in the next year and the next five years, ask yourself the following questions:

-What does my lifestyle look like?

-What are the emotions that I am feeling when hitting these goals?

-What are the challenges in the way of me hitting these goals?

-What can I do to overcome those challenges?

-What are my assets that I should leverage to hit those goals?

-What areas of my character development will help me reach those goals?

-What areas of my character will hinder me from reaching those goals?

-Visually, what are the things that I can see in the future once I hit those goals?

-Using my other senses, and imagining that I've hit those goals, what are the smells, the sounds, and the physical feelings that I have associated with those goals? In other words, what does the leather feel and smell like in your new Bentley as you're listening to your Pavarotti music on its CD player?

As a recruiter, you have to know where you are going. It's simple, but also critical. Whenever we were underway on the ship steering on a course heading, we were always off course. The wind, the seas, and the currents would always toss us about. In the same way, you will also have variables that you have no control over, knocking you about, pushing you away from your heading. But the key point is to at least have a heading and keep pushing to get back on track. At least with direction, you can focus straight ahead and know what course heading to steer toward.

Step Four: Create a Personal Success Journal

Your life is truly unique and special, and no one else has it. And it is worthy of being documented. So create a journal. Just go down to the Wal-Mart and buy a school composition notebook or even a cheap spiral notebook. Or if you want something nice buy a nice creamy-paged leather-covered journal from your local bookstore. Buy whatever motivates you to write. Just get one and start writing, darn it. This is one of the best decision-making tools you can add to your business book libraries. It is great for making decisions, for allowing your mind to flow freely about your future, for solving your problems, and for documenting your great and unique adventurous life. No one else will ever have a life like you and no one else ever has. Out of the billions of people that have walked the earth, there has never been nor ever will be another person just like you. You are truly unique and your life is worthy of being documented. Write about what issues are going on in your life. Write about your rejections, your hurts, your joys, and your frustrations with your desk. Write about specific experiences that you are excited about. Just write. Write often. Write everyday.

Many artists prefer writing first thing in the morning. This gets all the problems and demands of your day on paper. Write about whatever is going on in your life. It gets it down and out of the way, freeing your mind up to be creative. If you can take all the problems and challenges going on around you right now, put them down on paper, you can mentally allow yourself to come back to those problems and challenges, knowing that you won't forget about them because they're written down. Your subconscious mind will allow you to move on to other things. If it's written down, you can free your worrying up and focus on more solution-oriented issues.

A year ago I had a candidate who was considering making a move. He had left his current employer once before, came back to them again, and was considering leaving them again and joining my client. Naturally, I thought my client would be a better fit for him, and I really believed that, too. I wanted him to join my client. My client wanted him to join my client. Everybody was very, very interested in this candidate and we were all just biting our lips keeping from being too interested so we didn't scare him away. So finally, I told my client, "Whatever will be will be, we've done all we can do and we should just let the chips fall where they may."

I said to the candidate, "Why don't you just journal about this issue." I shared with him how powerful journaling had been in my own life. I told him about the time that I owned a staffing company and was grossly under funded and on the road to bankruptcy. I told him that I was tossing back and forth, telling myself that I should just keep on with it because I'd put so much in to it, and comparing that against the idea of cutting my losses and moving on; so I journaled all night long. I journaled until almost three o'clock in the morning and had concluded my decision-making exercise with something that gave me peace, which was to cut my losses and focus on my core competency. I think it's because I was so sincere and open with him that he was truly inspired to really listen to what I was telling him. I told him that I really didn't care what he did, as long as it was in his best interests. "Of course, I'd prefer you to join my client. That's how I make a living. But if you decide to stay there with your current company, I'm okay with that, too. I'm okay with that because more than collecting a fee, I care about you and I want to make sure that you make the absolute best decision. So take any obligation that you might feel toward me out of the equation, and just write. Write like a mad man. Write tonight when you get home about your feelings. Write about what would be the worst-case situation of you staying where you are and the worst-case situation about you joining my client. Write about the best-case situation for each scenario as well. You'll make the right decision, and whatever that is, I support you in it and will always consider you a friend. And when you're done writing, you'll know what to do."

So he did as I told him with his journal writing and decided to join my client. It really could have gone either way. What else could I have done? If I pushed him, he might have pushed back. If I did not push him and he decided to stay with his current company, he would probably have provided some very strong referrals; he might even have become an "evangelist" of my search abilities because I put my values ahead of profit motive. But he decided to join my client's organization and has been there ever since. Whew!

When you write, you can make decisions that will "stick" because your subconscious mind has already analyzed all the aspects of that decision. If you've never journaled before, I challenge you that in the next twenty-four hours to go out and purchase some sort of spiral notebook and start writing. Just get a pen and paper and start writing. And if you do this and don't feel it's worthwhile, call me up and tell me that I wasted your time. I can guarantee you this: if you start journaling, you will never ever stop. I still read through the journal of all of my tragedies when I was trying to grow my staffing and recruiting businesses. If anything, it gives me gratitude for how my life is today. And it gives me a historical baseline for what exactly I was going through. I've forgotten most of the details of things that have happened to me in my life. But when reading my journal, I am instantly catapulted back in time, vividly recalling the colors and sounds and smells of that particular time in my life…all because I took the time to document my experiences.

Step Five: Allow Yourself to be Successful

You are worthy of receiving the blessings that life has to offer. It took me years to figure that out. In order to be successful, you must feel like you are worthy of success. When I was in high school, I heard a youth leader talk about how money is the root of all evil and that none of us are worthy of anything that happens to us. At the time I thought this young man in his mid twenties was full of wisdom and character. But the more I grew in my own religious and spiritual life, the more I saw how flawed his thinking was. And because this guidance was flawed, I, too, had sabotaged ensuing ventures.

This baggage had remained with me for at least a decade and a half. It wasn't until my early thirties that I finally pulled out of this way of thinking, knowing that my Creator loves me and wants to bless me. When I pray, I don't just ask for His blessings; I ask for Him to help me feel worthy to receive His blessings as well. I ask for him to bless my efforts, to bless my work, and to increase my property. If you've ever read the small easy-to-read book The Prayer of Jabez, you know what I'm talking about. It's based on an Old Testament character that prayed for God to bless him, and to increase his property. And God did just that.

In the past, I have also tanked deals. I have kept my income at a certain level, subconsciously tanking deals or throwing money away because I just couldn't get my self-imposed income ceiling any higher than a certain level.

By developing this renewed sense of worth in your life, you will begin to feel worthy of success. I have literally seen people rise to the top of their careers and sabotage deals to quickly deflate their billings. I had a close friend in the industry that billed out over $300,000 in his first twelve months of production. And then he went nearly half a year without generating a single dime in revenue. Zero production. No retainers. No deals closed. Nothing at all. He subconsciously sabotaged his success. He had six or seven deals that were almost closed. The candidates had offers in hand, but the deals just weren't closed. We reviewed all of the deals that fell apart, and every reason was something that was in his control. I seriously suspect that for whatever reason, he subconsciously tanked the deals.

We all have a self-imposed income ceiling. There is a figure in your mind, whether you know it or not, that will determine how much you actually make in a year. If you go above that imaginary ceiling, you will tank your deals or fail to follow through on the important and simple aspects of the business. By reading books, listening to tapes, and associating with those at higher income levels, you'll eventually be able to push that income ceiling up higher and higher. All it takes is to break through those self-imposed beliefs that you have which limit your potential. Remember, you were designed for greatness and success.

Chapter Six

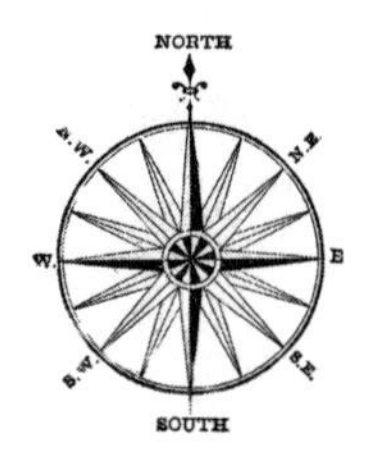

Let Fly the Spinnaker

The Attitude Turbo Charge

In high school, a friend of mine drove a Porsche. His dad was a wealthy doctor and gave him a beautiful sports car as a birthday gift when he was old enough to drive. My friend and I would drive all over town cruising in his gorgeous, shiny chick-magnet, listening to A Flock of Seagulls and Duran Duran on the cassette tape player. We would spend hours and hours driving around the Sonic after high school football games trying to get noticed. And the best way to get noticed was to catapult the vehicle from a state of inaction to that of incredible speed, and to do it rapidly; to change it from a state of potential energy to a state of movement and kinetic energy. And we didn't slowly accelerate. A very strong punch on the gas pedal increased its velocity along the highway. The energy of the vehicle was all within our control.

Your attitude is just like a Porsche. You have control over it. Is it inactive and negative? Or is your attitude positive and energized, adding speed and energy to your life? Regardless of your circumstances, you can catapult your attitude to a positive state in an instant.

When I was a youth and was involved in Boy Scouts, I would recruit friends of mine to join because it was so much fun. I recruited a friend of mine from my parish, Patrick, and I remember how he loved to go on the monthly camping trips.

On one camping trip, Patrick dove headfirst into a body of water without knowing how deep the pond was. He broke his neck and became paralyzed from the neck down. He was only fourteen years old.

My mom would take me to visit him in the hospital, and I couldn't stand seeing him there. I couldn't stand it at all. He was in a bed that would rotate his body from side to side so that the pressure of his body would be distributed evenly over his back, since he couldn't move anything except for the muscles on his face. He spent the entire day looking up at the ceiling. When he was awake, he would be staring at the same ceiling, day after day, month after month, and year after year. I cannot begin to comprehend how agonizing this was for his family, and I cannot even begin to understand how he could have made it as long as he did.

Patrick died just a few years later when we were both in our mid-teens. The whole experience of knowing him formed deep within me a desire to live a purposeful life. Because I knew Patrick and saw his situation, I made a commitment to live my life to the fullest, not letting a day escape me without experiencing a sense of loving others, passionately experiencing the bountiful gifts that God has given me, and being grateful for every single precious breath.

It is indeed possible to catapult your attitude from negative to positive instantly. I call it the Attitude Turbo Charge™. Your attitude certainly determines your outcome. Your sense of positive serendipity plays a large factor in the energy that you attract into your life. The challenge that we face as subjective, irrational, emotion-charged mammals, though, is to cope with disappointments and not let them influence our attitude.

The recruiter's career is filled with disappointments … almost every week, if not everyday. Candidates can do stupid things. And clients sometimes don't return phone calls and don't interview candidates in a timely manner, so your hot candidate moves on to another opportunity.

Clients could pay late, putting a damper on your cash flow. And sometimes you have a favorite client who leaves his employer and is replaced by someone who hates recruiters. Yes indeed, negative things are a big part of this business.

When I first got into sales, I was selling long distance for a major long distance carrier. At the time, I lived in Asheville, North Carolina, where I currently live. Our territory consisted of seventeen counties that included all of those far-away places in the boonies of Western North Carolina. I can honestly say that I was the top-producing sales rep for a seventeen-county region. There were two of us, and the other one wasn't very good.

It was brutal. I was kicked out of buildings, yelled at, screamed at and threatened. I had a product which was truly a commodity and wasn't very sexy. But I made it work. I learned how to sell. I actually was able to make a living above the poverty line. Each day I would say, "Today is going to be the greatest day of my life!" and it turned out to be. I still say that mantra each and every day.

On my way to work, I expect that today will bring wonderful surprises. I expect that people will just call me up out of the blue to give me their business; that people willingly return phone calls, that I always get through to the decision-maker because the secretaries are on my side.

I learned this attitudinal turbo-charging mechanism in the brutal world of long-distance sales. If you can make it in recruiting or in selling long distance, you can make it in anything. One way to definitely change your attitude immediately is to expect another outcome, a positive and serendipitous experience so fantastic that you get excited about the possibility. Expect your outcome to be a certain way, and it will.

If I am ever in the middle of a dire circumstance, one that seems to be hopeless, I instantly sit back, take a deep breath, and think of my friend Patrick. I think of Patrick's life, the fate that became his, and I feel encouraged knowing that he would probably want me to be grateful for my life. And at that point, my seemingly large problems don't seem very large anymore.

Chapter Seven

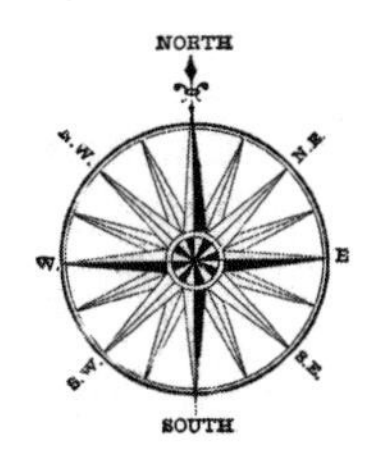

Where'd that Squall Come From?

Keeping a Sense of Humor in this Business

The summer before Sophomore year at Annapolis, known as Youngster Year, all midshipmen are expected to spend all but three or four weeks of their summer visiting Navy bases, riding ships, doing training, crawling through the mud at Quantico, flying in aircraft at Pensacola, and sailing around the world on warships. It's a great experience for midshipmen to really learn what the Fleet and the Marine Corps are like without the academic pressures of the school year clouding the mind. But it's very bad for the social life, especially if you have friends from high school back at your hometown.

For part of my youngster cruise, I was able to get a slot on a six-week sailing cruise down to the Bahamas. Now, a sailing cruise as a midshipman on a sailboat is very different than one that you might take once you start making money. You don't get swing lessons, you don't get gourmet food, and you don't have Doc and Gopher running around the deck of the ship. For my cruise, we sailed from Annapolis, down to the Bahamas and back; all on a forty-four-foot sail boat, three feet above the raging sea. Being at sea level in the stormy Atlantic gives you a real appreciation for nature. Technology can't save you if you get in a mess and nobody knows where you are except your fellow crewmembers. It is something I remember very fondly, and probably will never do again.

Our voyage was very exciting, especially for a nineteen year old away from home. We stopped at Norfolk, Charleston, Fort Lauderdale, Miami, and the Bahamas, taking time to visit clubs, meet local girls, and appreciate the under-21 drinking age at that time. (Responsibly, of course.)

During our voyage we saw some very unique things, such as sea turtle, schools of porpoise and dolphin, flying fish, whales, and sharks. There's nothing more frightening and exhilarating than seeing a whale break through the surface of the water and crash back in to the sea... three feet away from you. Flying fish would hit us in the back, landing on the deck of the boat as they skimmed across the sea. And around Cape Hatteras, a notoriously violent sea because of the mixing of northern and southern waters, we saw some action. On our return trip north, the seas were extremely calm because the wind was so strong that it cut the waves in half. With wind speeds of over fifty miles an hour, the seas were easy to navigate, even with our smallest sails hoisted on the mast. I was at the helm, decked out in all the foul weather gear that I could find, making everyone harness themselves in the boat. Everyone's face was buried in their hands to keep the bruising waters and winds from blinding them...except for me. I was the helmsman, and needed to steer the ship. It was one of the most exciting experiences of my life, steering the ship north to safety through a passing storm that just moments before had waves up to twenty feet. The weather can change in an instant on the sea, and you must always be ready. After my watch was over and I went below to have a cup of hot chocolate, I realized that my face was sore. My face was sore for the next few days because of the sensational wind bruising my face with the sea.

Around Cape Hatteras on our initial voyage, things were even more exciting. We took a detour through the Intercoastal Waterway, trying to avoid the bad weather and wind funnels (tornadoes) that had been sighted very near us. And things had appeared to be safe. The wind was calm; we were all decked out in shorts, Ray Bans, our docksider shoes, and the best suntan oil that money could buy. And I looked ahead at the other two ships in our party, about a quarter mile ahead of us. The first one was sailing along, and all of a sudden its mast slammed into the ocean, with its sails touching the water, and then up righted itself. About thirty seconds later, I saw the mast of the ship directly in front of us slam into the ocean, with its sails touching the water. And thirty seconds later, we were all jolted to the starboard side of the boat as our own boat catapulted towards the port side, slamming our mast and sails into the sea, quickly up righting and steadying itself as if nothing had ever happened!

"Where did THAT come from?" we all asked at the same time (censored for publishing, of course). It took us by surprise, as if it were acting following the storyboard from a bad Hemingway novel. From out of nowhere a squall had sent our ship flying, filling the dinner pots cooking on the stove with cool and fresh seawater. And we saw our shipmate who was cooking dinner surface from below, wearing the spaghetti that just moments before was waiting to be eaten. And we just couldn't help but laugh. Not just a chuckle, but a unified pirate-like guttural strong healthy laugh. The adrenaline subsiding, we all kind of sat down and shook it off, each helping to clean up the small galley and find some sort of dry food to cook.

You're going to have similar things happen to you in the search business, but at least you don't have to wear rain gear in your office. Surprises are going to develop a life force of their own, as if they were trying to shatter your positive attitude. You will be pushed to the brink of breaking down because of the tragedy that will come after you with a vengeance. Candidates who seemed strong will get weak knees and take counteroffers. Clients who at one point were close to you will become distant. And sometimes people will lie to you. Don't expect it. Don't act like it's going to happen. Just don't be surprised if it does. And if it does, shake it off, clean up the galley, and keep on sailing. And develop a sense of humor about it.

When I first started in the business, my manager taught me everything I knew. I'll call my mentor "Jim" because, well, that was his name. Jim came from Pittsburgh. Just looking at him gave you a sense somehow that he survived some very cold winters.

Jim taught me to keep a humor file. A humor file is a collection of bodacious resumes, jaw dropping emails, and funny business articles. Now, I'm not very organized, but I do have priorities. And when it comes to doing something that's really fun or feels good, I make it a priority. Just like every other recruiter. Shoot, that's why we're in sales and recruiting because it sure beats working for a living. When you're in sales and you have the right attitude and you can sell like a freaking animal, then it's a blast.

So I set up a humor file.

One thing I never thought to do until recently, though, was to set up a spite file. Now, I'm a very spiteful person in a silly sort of way. Sometimes experiences that I have with losers bother me, so I replay them in my mind with all sorts of vivid colors and music and exaggerated caricatures to help me take the sting out of bad moments. That's one of the tricks that top performers learn when they get upset. Don't take it so seriously. (By the way, that's an NLP trick. Neuro Linguistic Programming is a way that you can train your mind to enhance or decrease the associations that you have with certain experiences.) Now, my spite file doesn't really exist. I don't think I would admit it even to my subconscious mind that I would take the time and effort to set up a spite file. Doing something like that would seem so...so...spiteful. And that's truly in bad form. Spiteful people are bad dressers and drive crappy cars and don't make any money. Plus, they don't go to many parties because they have bad breath and no friends.

But nevertheless, there is a hint of spite on the outward skin of my heart. Spite is kind of like a grape that is about to ferment. It looks good for a little while, but throw that thing away because it sure has no purpose. Look at it briefly, but get it in the trashcan.

Five or six years ago a client of mine, a large, well known, privately owned company from the northeast, was opening an office in Florida. They were in the process of staffing it up, so they hired my firm to find some mid-level line managers for their office. I liked the company and the decision-makers I was working with, so I thought I would like to recruit on the assignment.

I worked for a week or so on the assignment, and came up with a shortlist of finalists. One of the finalists was "Bob."

Bob was a nice guy, a real nice guy. He was a very talented individual with a degree from a reputable New England university. He was complete with Yankee accent. Perfect for the transplanted northerners.

My client loved Bob. Their clients loved Bob. Bob was the man. I checked the references, and the references were glowing.

The next step, then, is to verify the degree. No problem. Verifying degrees is very easy. You just call up the main switchboard at the university, ask to talk to the people who verify degrees, and say that you'd like to verify the degree of someone for employment purposes. The college worker will give you the info, and that's that. I called Bob, told him I was going to verify his degree and asked for his social security number to verify his degree. He gave me the social security number to verify the degree. So I told him I was going to verify the degree, a formality, and once the degree was verified then I'd be back in touch to get the offer from my client once we verified the degree. He seemed real excited about the offer and seemed okay with me verifying his degree because verifying the degree is something that a good recruiter or employer will do, that is, to verify the degree. So, here I go. I'm calling to verify the degree. I'm dialing to verify the degree. I reach the switchboard of the university to verify the degree, and I ask the receptionist to transfer me to the people who verify the degrees. "Verify the degree, sir? One moment, please, while I connect you to the people who verify the degrees.

"Records."

"Yes, I need to verify the degree of a graduate of your school."

"Name?"

"Bob Theliar."

"Year graduated?"

"19XX."

"One moment, sir. Let me put you on hold." I hold. I hold. I hold. They come back.

"Sir?"

"Yes," I respond. I can tell by the way she said, "Sir?" that something was up. Anytime you think something's up, something's up. Trust your instincts.

"Sir, we have a record of Bob Theliar attending our school, but not having a degree."

"Oh, gee, there must be some mistake. Can you check again? I'm looking at it right here on his resume and it says he has a Bachelors of Whatever degree in such and such."

"Well, sir, we do have his name attending classes, but not graduating."

Gee, there must be something wrong with their records. How on earth could this have happened? There must be some mistake!

I frantically tried to reach Bob at his current employer's office. Not there. I try him on his cell phone. No answer. I call him at his house. Answer: his wife, his very pleasant sweet-sounding wife.

"Hello?"

"Yes, Jeanie? Jeanie? My name is Scott Love..." and I give her the background on the search and that,

"Bob's degree isn't checking out and obviously there must be some mistake because records are often jumbled and mumbled when they transfer them from old moldy dusty rusty antiquated record books which are filled with mistakes anyway and after all it's just clumsy half-drunk college students who work in the registrar's office anyways and who knows how many mistakes they make and I'm sure it must be some mistake...but have Bob call me right away so we can square away this whole mess, which I'm sure isn't his fault, and I'm not calling your husband a liar at all. No ma'am, I'm not even implying that or hinting at it or making any sort of inference or not even thinking about it ...because you and I both know that you think you've been married to a college graduate for all these years."

"Okay, sweetie, I'll have Bob call you when he gets back home from *woik,*" she sang to me in her sweet New England accent.

At this point, I didn't know what was up. I actually believed that his degree was real. After all, it said it on the resume. It was right there looking up at me with puppy dog eyes and a sweet smile on its face: Bachelors of Whatever degree in Such and Such. "Yes, I'm real!" it cried out. "Believe in me! I exist! I am real!" Yes, I believe in you, my sweet resume. I believe in you. I'll always believe in you, because you're in ink and whatever's in ink must be true. If it's printed on paper, then it's got to be true because I'm only in my twenties. (Note to reader: I'm not cynical, I swear. Just wise. I think wisdom hit me like a pie truck when all of this happened.)

The phone rang.

"Good afternoon, Scott Love speaking."

"Don't you EVER talk to my wife about anything like that again. If you want to talk about that, you talk to me, okay?"

"Bob, wha...wha...wha...calm down. What are you talking about?"

"You leave my wife out of this, you hear!" he screamed with a uniquely frantic intensity.

"Wha...wha...wha...what are you talking about?"

"What are you doing talking to my wife about this degree business?" he said, sounding like a very believable mobster impersonator. I was expecting him to say something that included the phrase *"breaka yo legs"*.

"Bob, I'm on your side," I responded, sounding a bit like an understanding psychologist. "I called the school, they said they had a record of you attending, but no degree. I'm sure the degree isn't checking out and obviously there must be some mistake because records are often jumbled and mumbled when they transfer them from old dusty moldy rusty antiquated record books which are filled with mistakes anyway and after all it's just clumsy half-drunk college students who work in the registrar's office anyway and who knows how many mistakes they make and I'm sure it must be some mistake...but I'm glad you called me right away so we can square away this whole mess which I'm sure isn't your fault and I'm not calling you a liar at all no sir I'm not even implying that or hinting at it nor making any sort of inference or not even thinking about it ...because you and I both know that you've had this degree printed on your resume after all these years."

"Scott, I gotta level with you." Translation: I'm full of cow manure. "Scott, I gotta level with you. I don't have a degree." Funny. The earth didn't exactly stop turning at that moment. I remember kind of stretching and yawning when he said that, kind of like it didn't really surprise me too much.

"But, Bob, your resume says you have a degree."

"Scott! I don't have one."

"Bu...bu...bu...but it's right here on your resume. How...how...how...how on earth did it get on your resume if you don't have a degree?"

"I just don't have one, okay?"

Okay, Bob. Sure. Make me look like a freaking idiot in front of my client who loved you so much. Kind of like I'm the matchmaker bringing a transvestite to the wedding and not knowing about it until the garter toss. This is going to be one really awkward phone call when I tell my client this.

I call my client. I tell him about the situation, and that I have backup candidates and that we should forget about Bob.

"You know what, Scott?" my client said. "I like Bob. Our clients like Bob. Bob is the man. We're going to hire Bob."

"Bu...bu...bu...but I have other candidates and I'd be glad to..."

"Forget about it, Scott. We'll hire Bob. Let's make him an offer."

I can't really remember too much about what he said at that point because I was busy documenting the phone call in case, for some reason, my client ever tried to sue me for this. So Bob was hired and started with my client.

A few months later, I thought it would be good to visit my client. I spent a good many hours with everyone in the office there, and got to know the client and the staff that I placed in the office. What a good group of people. Even Bob seemed to be a decent fellow. Perhaps my standards were unrealistic. Perhaps I was being too judgmental and too critical on him. After all, he almost finished his degree. Maybe "Bachelors of Whatever" translates into "Almost Finished Degree." Maybe they should come up with AFD (standing for Almost Finished Degree) along with BS and BA. Bob Theliar, AFD.

I kept in touch with my client and the staff over the next year, and things seemed to be going well.

And then one day... I get a call from Bob. He's no longer employed with my client.

"What happened, Bob?"

"Things didn't work out."

Now, I've been in this business long enough to know that when you hear "Things didn't work out," it translates into "I got fired but don't want to admit it." So Bob asked me if I had anything out there in the Florida market. Sure, Bob. Hold on a minute. Let me check my files. Looking...looking...looking...nope. I don't see anything on my search list for people with the degree designation of AFD.

"No, Bob, I don't have anything right now. But I'll call you (social untruth so I don't end up with a stalker with a grudge on my hands) if I come across something."

"Hey," he said, sounding just like Fonzie, only without the coolness. "Hey, thanks a lot, buddy. Can I fax you my resume? I updated it."

"Err, sure, Bob. That would be...um...nice."

So, the conversation ended, and Bob faxed me his updated resume. I read it, and yes, he did update the resume with my client's information on it. And remaining on the resume was the same fake degree that he falsified years before. He forgot that this recruiter caught him in a lie, and he thought he could continue to lie to the rest of the world.

I lost touch with Bob. He's probably out there working for some company that doesn't check degrees. And the sad thing is that his wife still probably thinks she's married to a college graduate. Not graduating from college is not really a big deal. Pretending like you have graduated from college is, though, and this habit of dishonesty will probably be repeated in other areas of his life. We are all the same person twenty-four hours a day. We're the same person at work that we are at home. It's not like you're going to be honest at home and dishonest at work. If you're dishonest, you'll be dishonest in many areas of your life. And if you lie about your degree, you'll lie about other things too.

I feel bad for people like Bob, people who think they're never going to get "found out" about their little lies. Even though it's a little lie, it sends a very large tacky neon red flag to the universe that this person cannot be trusted in big things. If you can't be trusted in little things, you can't be trusted in big things.

People like Bob don't bother me anymore. The universal laws of reaping and sowing will catch up with him, I'm sure. I don't know how things were in your trailer park growing up, but when I was a kid, we always heard the phrase "what goes around comes around".

Poor Bob. If only he'd been smart enough to change his ways once he'd been caught.

Keep a sense of humor and expect things to get weird in this business. Watch out for those surprise squalls, and watch out for those fake degrees.

Chapter Eight

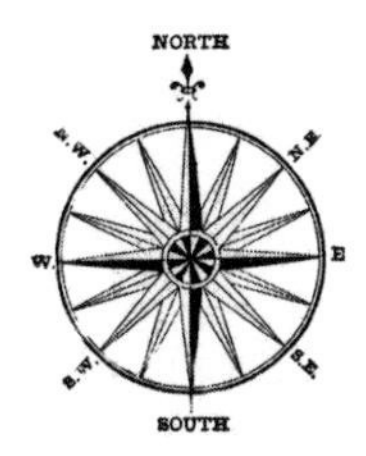

Charting Your Course

Strategic Goal Setting for Recruiters

Writing down goals is one of the easiest ways to guarantee the probability of you being successful, yet so many of us just fail to do this. And if it is done, the goal is usually forgotten and usually filed away in some manila folder, never to be seen or heard from again.

Lay in your course to where you are headed. Write in your Personal Success Journal where you want to be in both five years and one year. That is all you can really focus on.

Forget about all the other complex goal-setting matrices that you've ever heard about. Just focus on five and one year goals, and that's it. The two year, three year and four year goals will reveal themselves to you at the proper time; just like you were driving a car, all you have to do is worry about your final destination and the cars that are immediately in front of you. You'll figure out that merging scenario at the exit five miles ahead of you when you get there. Don't worry about that situation right now. Just focus on the cars immediately in front of you and the directions to the final destination.

In creating your five and one year goals, think in terms of those areas of your life that matter most. Remember that to be successful as a recruiter you must strive for balance. Balance is key, because it allows you not to just be fulfilled, but also to be more effective on your desk. Stress management is all about contraction and release. Contraction and release. Contraction and release. And by having a well-rounded life, you allow the stresses and pressures of your desk to be released, and to return, and to release, and to return. Contraction and release. It also creates a more fulfilling life for you, a life that you can eagerly share with those who you love.

When you write those five and one-year goals, divide them into categories. What categories are important to you? When drafting this list, call it the Life Goals List™. Find out what's important in your life, and set a goal around it. Some ideas include the following:

Business Goals

Production/Billing Goals

Recreational Goals

Family Goals

Mental/Educational Goals

Spiritual Goals

Physical/Athletic Goals

Financial Goals

Business goals can include any sort of business related activities outside of your recruiting desk. Perhaps it is future consulting with a client, or adding a researcher or recruiters to your team. What are the business areas that you see yourself achieving in five years, and also one year?

Production/Billing Goals are critical. Think of the number that you want to hit in five years. Think of the number that you want to hit this year. And focus on that number all the time. Commit it to memory. Measure your production against that number every time you close a deal. I even created one of those thermometers, kind of like the ones the United Way has whenever they have a fund-raiser. And every time I close a deal, I color in the red "mercury", showing myself visibly getting closer to my annual billing goals. I honestly don't think about my other goals every day. I don't go nuts over how many books I want to read every year, even though I have it in writing. I go crazy, though, over my production number. I become obsessed with my production number and think about it all the time. It becomes sort of like a very bad gambling habit, and I just can't quit thinking about it.

Recreational Goals are very important and are too often neglected, and they actually contribute to the bottom line. A few years ago, my wife and I went to a charity fundraiser for my parish. Many items were available for sale, including golf outings, professional services, and vacation packages. All of the proceeds were given away to local charities such as Habitat for Humanity and local women's shelters. It was toward the end of the evening, when everyone was tired and had spent all of their money, when a weeklong vacation package at one of Cabo San Lucas' finest resorts was on the auction block. It was a five star resort called Club Cascadas, right on the beach of Cabo San Lucas on the southernmost tip of The Baja Peninsula in Mexico. I could sense that everyone just seemed too tired to raise his or her hands. Many people had left for the evening, and my wife and I impulsively decided to bid on the item. The bidding started at $500 for the week. The rental unit had its own pool and Jacuzzi and had a retail rental price of about $450 per night. We ended up getting the entire week, right smack in the prime of the fishing season there, for a total of only $750.00. It was our first vacation since our honeymoon that didn't involve relatives or in-laws. Vacations are for losers; I used to think. And then we went to Cabo and sat on the beach reading novels and drinking silly drinks. I didn't even think about work starting on my third day there. It also helped being at a resort with no in-room telephones. And I couldn't figure out how to operate the pay phones, so fortunately I blew off checking my voicemail. We went to art galleries, walked on the beach holding hands, explored surrounding little villages, and ate some of the best food I've ever had. And at the end of the week, I was ready to go home. I wasn't anxious about getting to my desk. I was just ready for it. And I came back relaxed, refreshed, and re-energized.

Write down your recreational goals, and perhaps have a reward system attached. Don't go out and buy an RV with one deal that you might close. Instead, take your spouse out to dinner. Keep your rewards way below your budget, and make them fun. Get the whole family involved in your recreational rewards. And set distinct recreational goals on top of your rewards. Turn off the television and spend that time recreating with your loved ones. Life isn't long enough to allow for pathetic reruns of The Jeffersons, Laverne and Shirley and other great hallmarks of television to take up your time. Don't just spend your time doing recreational things...invest your time doing recreational things. By spending it with others who you love, you are investing in relationships.

Family Goals can tie in to these recreational goals. I'd strongly recommend developing a hobby or an area of "fun concentration", perhaps an activity that your whole family can take an interest in. Some ideas include themes for your activities such as visiting local historic monuments, Civil War battlefields, National Parks, NASCAR racetracks, baseball stadiums, art galleries, or whatever you and your family have in common. It could be creating scrapbooks or playing some sort of sport or game. For my little toddler, it's visiting the Health Adventure in Asheville, a museum geared toward little kids with an impressive toddler play area. It's right next to an art gallery, so it has something for our whole family.

Some of the family goals I've developed in my own life include offering to help out with chores, giving out more hugs, saying only kind words, and praying for my family. It can be as simple as giving an affectionate touch to your spouse so many times a day or turning your house into a home of love and affection. Once you write that down as a goal, your subconscious mind begins to seek ways for you to grow in that area.

Mental and Education Goals keep you fresh. For this I would recommend adopting the mentality of a perpetual student. Develop specific areas of your profession in which you would like to grow, and start reading books on them. Attend recruiting seminars when they come to town. Join your state and national association and attend their meetings and conferences. If I come to your town, I would invite you to attend my seminar. It's geared toward direct-hire recruiters, and the schedule of my seminars is at www.recruitingmastery.com. Seek out other respected trainers and speakers; both in the recruiting industry and those that have good general sales knowledge or inspiring messages they can share.

Ask yourself how many books you are reading right now, and double it; well, unless you're not reading any, because zero times two is still zero. So increase it to one book a month, hot shot, and double it the next month. Get a Barnes and Noble bookseller discount card and become a maniac about reading. Read books on motivation and selling and recruiting. The appendix has a list of recommended reading for you.

Begin a tape and video library of training. I have purchased just about every tape-training product within the recruiting industry that has ever been made. Some are great and some are good. Get everything. Invest a percentage of your billings back into yourself. If your manager won't do it for you, do it for yourself. You are totally responsible for training yourself, not your manager. The owner and manager of your company shouldn't care as much about your training as you should for yourself. If you truly desire to be a champion, you will develop your own personal library of information, and refer to it over and over and over again. Highlight the books. Review and re-review the videotapes. I personally review the most elementary videotapes of the recruiting business every single year, at least once a year. And I learn new things from it. Or if I don't learn anything new, at least I'm reminded to stop being so sloppy and to focus on the basics. Your education in the business should be a priority. And if you aren't training, remember one thing: your competition is. Take time to sharpen the saw, as Dr. Stephen Covey says, and train and retrain.

Spiritual Goals are important, because we are all spiritual beings. My grandmother used to tell me that we are not spiritual beings in a physical world…we are physical beings in a spiritual world. By developing a deep conviction in your faith, you develop a guiding viewpoint on how you perceive reality. I grew up in the Episcopal Church, and my faith was a very strong and stable force in my life as a child. I've learned to seek my Lord's guidance in all areas of my life. I view my business and my finances with a spiritual perspective. My family holds that perspective at the center of our marriage and our family life. You'll probably never see me standing on a street corner holding a sign with a Bible verse on it. And I'm probably one of the biggest sinners that you'll ever meet, which is probably why I fervently and passionately seek my Lord each and every day. Whatever decisions you come up with in your own life, however you choose to seek that path, I hope that you can develop as much depth and peace in your own spiritual journey that I've been able to find. I have a resource that I can run to in times of trouble. I have strength to continue in spite of the harshest of circumstances. And I have peace that goes well beyond my own understanding. Whatever you choose to do, I respect you. Start asking those questions and you'll start finding the answers that you need. All you need to do, though, if you've never even thought of anything like this before, is to ask.

Some of the goals you can develop for yourself, regardless of your faith, might include fellowshipping with others, praying, meditating, reading, or simply journaling on spiritual issues.

If you don't have **physical goals**, you are neglecting one of the most important areas of your life. I never liked sports.

I have never watched a complete football or baseball game on television...ever. That even includes the Super Bowl and the World Series. But I love to work out. (Well...at least I love to finish working out. Starting is the hardest part.) I don't compete competitively in sports and don't really have any desire to. But if you start exercising, you will feel better about yourself, you'll have more energy, and you'll be more relaxed. That relaxed state of being is the essence of success, and by exercising, you'll be able to increase your productivity.

Here's the disclaimer: seek guidance from a physician before you begin an exercise regime. There, I've said it to cover myself. And also read **Body for Life** by Bill Phillips and Michael D'Orso. Their book is an excellent overview for someone who has never exercised before and for the intermediate workout enthusiast. And if you're not ready to start lifting and running, then start walking. Write down how many times per week you'd like to take a walk, and how far you would like to go. Physically write down what exercises you hope to accomplish that week and document your success. Not only will you feel good, you'll feel good about yourself. Working a desk as a recruiter is definitely one of the worst professions for your health because you're sitting at a desk all day on the telephone. If you're not on the telephone then you're not doing your job. And because you're just sitting there all day, it's easy to get lazy. Plus the Twinkies. Oh my gosh, the Twinkies and the Twix bars and the ice cream sandwiches and the...well, you get the picture. Yes, sitting on your bottom all day seems to encourage the devouring of chocolate and sweets.

After you've checked with your physician, write down simple exercise goals. If you have to, hire a personal trainer to give you instruction. You don't have to use a personal trainer for every workout. You can have them spend an hour with you and give you an overview, or meet less frequently. Take care of yourself because you're the only self that you'll ever get.

It means absolutely nothing to be a big biller and have nothing to show for it. Don't spend everything you earn. Set monthly **financial goals.** How much are you going to give to charities? How much are you going to save? How much debt are you intending to pay off? Probably the best thing I ever did was to have my financial planner set up an automatic debit from my checking account. Every month, a certain amount is taken from my checking account for investment purposes and put in to an investment program. It happens on the 22nd of the month. I set up this transaction automatically in my Quicken program that I use for my personal finances. If this weren't automatically done for me, I would probably blow it off because I'm so lazy! Hooray again for technology!

One of the saddest things in the world is to see someone who at one time was making money but who spent more than they produced. Live below your means. And if you want to make a regular impact in the world, make sure you decide what percentage of your net income you are going to give to charities.

Do you have your five and one year Life Goals written down? Good! Way to go, champion! The next step is to look thirty days out. That's it. Forget about nine month, six month and three month goals. Just focus on the next thirty days. Now, part of me says, yes, it's important to have quarterly production goals. But I really don't believe most recruiters have the inherent ability to think long term, that why so many of us have the bad habit of spending everything that we make. I've met recruiters who claimed to be $600,000 a year producers but who were flat broke because they literally wore their retirement. They would spend all of their money on areas that didn't produce a return, such as expensive suits, jewelry, ties, shirts, and platinum cufflinks for their fancy French cuff silk shirts. They couldn't see past the next meal or the next deal in front of them. (Note: Put at least ten percent of what you earn in some sort of retirement account. Even if it's a money market account or savings, just put it aside because some day you'll be old and not able to work anymore and if you don't start today, you'll never start. That's a challenge to you if you haven't done that before. By the end of the week, I challenge you to start a program of putting at least ten percent of your W-2 into some sort of an investment program).

I can certainly empathize with not being able to see beyond thirty days. So let's just not fight it and admit that we all have a hard time looking past the next month. You know where you're going in five years, right? You have your one-year goal written down, correct? Good. Now let's break it down into monthly pieces.

Chapter Nine

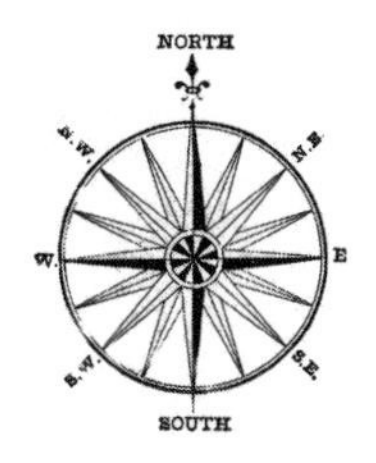

Bite Sized Pieces

The Monthly System for Recruiting Success

Each month is your yardstick on your way to success. I have read many books on goal setting, listened to tapes, and been to seminars, and usually forget about everything I learn within a month or so. Some of the systems I've seen are too complex with too many variables to count, too much to measure. All of those variables are usually forgotten and I then fall back into the old way of doing things. Maybe it's just that I'm too lazy. Just like any recruiter or salesperson, if it is fun or feels good, I can usually follow up on it. But if it takes too much effort, then forget about it. I'm off to having a good time doing something else. So I'd like to share with you a very simple system of success for reaching your goals. It's easy, fun and something that you can start immediately, which will help you maintain your focus and accountability.

I have seen some systems which measure everything from the number of dialed attempts, completed calls, completed successful calls, completed unsuccessful calls, completed successful calls which result in a meeting or an interview, the number of times you scratch yourself, and a host of other variables to determine whether or not a recruiter is successful. This type of system can be effective yet complex. This type of system usually serves the manager rather than the recruiter. It gives the manager a comfort level that the recruiter is actually making the calls that he or she is supposed to be making, which really isn't a bad way to measure it at all. If you work for a search firm or staffing company that has call accounting (SMDR) built into their system, then by all means, take advantage of that technology. By seeing how many times you dial the phone and how many times you are actually connected to someone, you can see what sort of frequency you have as far as your dial ratio goes.

Other systems focus on the number of calls a recruiter makes and breaks that down by the type of call, such as a recruiting call or marketing call. This is probably a great way for a beginner to establish good habits and patterns in the business. In fact, it is probably a good way that any experienced veteran recruiter can have himself or herself held accountable to their employer. The only problem with this, though, is that experienced veteran recruiters loathe accountability. They would rather work an intuitive desk and not have any sort of accountability. I believe that there are arguments on both sides of this debate that are valid. But the bottom line is this: are you producing? And not only are you producing, but are you producing at your fullest maximum potential? That is the single most important question that needs to be answered by both the recruiter and the recruiting manager. Not just the performance, but the maximum performance limit must be measured. What is the maximum performance limit, what is the actual performance, and what is the delta (the difference) between the two. Once those three variables can be established, a baseline can be set for performance goal-setting for the recruiter.

In focusing on your thirty-day program, there are two primary areas of concentration for goal setting. The first area is to focus on each of the categories that I mentioned in the last chapter, to focus on your Life Achievement Goals. The second area is to focus on your performance.

Keep in mind that you are totally in control of all aspects of your performance. The number of connects you make has nothing to do with the economy. Alan Greenspan doesn't keep you from making another call at the end of the day. Neither does your boss or your neighbor in the cube next to you or anyone else you can think of to blame your problems on. It's all up to you.

I will admit that the economy in the early part of the new decade has been an obstacle to many recruiters, especially those in sectors where technology is the main focus. I've had friends who were big-billing 600K recruiters have their entire businesses dwindle to almost nothing. That does indeed seem to be one sector that has almost dried up at the time of this printing.

But there are those recruiters in that technology niche that are doing quite well. And there are others in more standard traditional niches that have seen an increase in spite of a bad economic time for the country. It is entirely feasible to increase your production when the rest of the country is in a recession. I know that my own personal production increased by over twenty-percent in 2002, and I moved both my business and my family across the country and stopped working my desk in the fourth quarter to focus on my speaking business. I far surpassed my entire 2001 in the first three quarters of 2002. How I did this was simple: I stopped blaming the economy for my poor production. I got so sick and tired of hearing whining recruiters blame the economy that I decided to create my own economy. It was an economy of wealth. It was an economy of a high level of value to my clients. It was the type of economy that lived between my ears and was a land filled with buried treasure. And all it took was a decision. I sat down at the beginning of 2002 and said that I was going to take control of my desk and do what was not possible. And to tell you the truth, most of my success was in the decision, more so than the action. I think that if you have the guts to stand up and say "I choose not to participate in this recession!", then you, too, will realize an increased production when everyone else around you is stunned by the lack of work.

By taking control of your performance goals and monitoring them on a daily basis, you can outpace the economy. By becoming sharper and more focused and better at recruiting, you will pass those who choose not to read books on their industry, those who choose not to invest in themselves through training products, and those who are not willing to do whatever it takes to succeed. I guess it's sort of like those documentaries filmed on the wilderness of Africa. Someone's going to get eaten by the lion, and it's not the fastest antelope. It's the weaker ones who aren't paying attention to the dangers around them. Or maybe they were lingering around the watering hole a little bit longer than they should have and they became easy prey. Someone's going to get eaten by the lion. Is that going to be you?

It is all about choice. You do not have to do whatever it takes, and that's fine. But if you choose to have the life of true achievement and professional fulfillment, you will learn to become a disciplined maniac about following the progress of your performance goals.

In looking at the most elemental aspect of the recruiting business, nobody makes a dime until a placement occurs. That, of course, is how we all make a living. Whether it's contingency or retained, the placement is the end result. It's the objective.

If you are new to this business, you will learn to master the art or determining and following your ratios. If you are a veteran, I can almost hear you nodding enthusiastically about this. And the ratios are what make it a predictable business.

Think about this business: you are creating something from nothing. You happen to get a search from a client looking for some type of individual. And you happen to find that exact type of individual. You present the candidate, facilitate the offer, and close the deal. Imagine the odds of everything going right! Astronomical. But somehow you make it work out. And if you do it enough with a persistent plan, good work habits, and the ability to ethically influence others, it becomes a predictable business. It becomes the type of business that can be measured. And what can be measured can be improved, and that is why we measure ratios.

The most important ratio to track is the number of interviews to the number of ensuing placements: How many candidates have to interview before an offer is given and accepted. Other ratios include the number of candidate presentations, the number of interviews (send outs), the number of offers, the number of turndowns, the number of acceptances, and the number of candidates who start. But the real three areas on which to focus your energies are the number of candidate presentations, the interviews, and the acceptances.

If you do this business properly you don't have to worry about turndowns or counteroffers. In fact, you can go several years without getting a single turndown or a single counteroffer. Years ago, when I was learning how to play golf, I would read books on the game. Arnold Palmer wrote one book that made an impact on me. Arnie was writing about the wind as a variable to the accuracy of the flight of the golf ball, and said that if you hit the ball the way it is supposed to be hit, then the wind does not affect the flight of the golf ball all that much. Instead of worrying about the wind, you should focus your mind on a good swing and the proper hitting of the ball. It's very similar to counteroffers and turndowns. If you just focus on managing the search process, counteroffers and turndowns won't be an issue anymore.

In my other book, The Recruiter's Compass! Your Complete Guide To Finding Buried Treasure in the World of Recruiting. I give specific detailed verbiage on how to communicate to candidates and clients to almost guarantee that you will get a 100% acceptance and a 100% counteroffer diffusal, should a counteroffer be given to a candidate. In my tape series, "Zero Defect Counteroffers", I give specific detailed information on the twelve steps to kissing counteroffers goodbye forever. Both of these products can be ordered directly from my secure website, www.recruitingmastery.com. To summarize the theory behind those ratios, I establish control with the candidate, which is really legitimate influence and leadership, from the very beginning, and during the qualifying call, I determine whether or not the candidate is susceptible to accepting a counteroffer from an employer. Because of the values clarification in my own life, I am congruent in how I do business and I usually can portray myself with enough sincerity over the phone to gain the trust of the candidate and develop a real relationship of authenticity, which is covered in detail in chapter ten. That, together with the recruiter's verbiage and scripting of the offer and counteroffer prep process, can usually win them over and make sure that if an offer is given, it is accepted and stays accepted.

For clarification, I'm offering the following definitions. A **"candidate presentation"** is when a recruiter either physically faxes or emails a candidate's resume to a client. Don't track verbal presentations. You can verbally present a candidate to a client that doesn't have a need for such an animal. But when the client says, "Yes, I might be interested in looking at her resume", then chalk it up on the board as a candidate presentation.

The **"interview"** is the actual conversation between a client and a candidate. For my own tracking purposes, I count telephone conversations that are scheduled interviews and which last longer than thirty minutes. I consider that a true evaluation between the client and candidate and give it the same merit as an actual face-to-face interview. Different search firms might not consider the telephone call as an "interview" and might add another category for tracking the ratios. I do not consider a quick **"phone screen"** as an interview in my tracking process. Only if it is a real evaluation do I consider it in my ratios.

Long ago the term "send out" entered our industry. In my fifth year in the business I finally figured out why it was called a "send out". In the early days of the business, when the applicant (now called a candidate) paid the fee, the applicant would physically go to the employment agency and apply in person for positions. He or she would be sitting at the recruiter's desk and the recruiter would call companies marketing the candidate. If the employer indicated that they had a need and an interest, the recruiter would send out the candidate to the employer. Hence, the phrase, "send out." That phrase seems to still be in use today, but I've heard it used as an interview, a candidate presentation, and a telephone screen.

Let's look at how you should track these goals on a monthly basis. First, set a goal for the number of placements you want to occur. This is determined by how much revenue you want, what your average fee is for your office, and how experienced you are. In other words, what's your track record? What has been your interview to placement ratio in the past twelve months? For my office, which would have rookie recruiters doing mostly contingency search for mid-level positions, our fee size would be between $15,000 and $25,000 for a novice. The interview to placement ratio for a novice recruiter with a selling background would be around 5:1 for tracking purposes. That would mean that for every five interviews that took place, one placement would occur. It might take thirty candidate presentations to get five interviews for a recruiter. Sometimes the ratio might be 7:I or 6:I, depending on the experience level of the recruiter. But we always used the 5:I ratio for an office average. Once you have become experienced, or if you get into high level retained search work, you'll see your ratios get to 4:I or 3:I. The key is to keep the candidate flow the same, get the ratios better through training, and increase your production. So, if you're a novice recruiter looking at a 6:I ratio, you might present thirty candidates and yield six interviews, with one of those six interviews resulting in a single placement. Your ratio status would be 30: 6: I. Once you develop your skill level at the business, specifically the phases of the interview preparation and interview debriefs and offer negotiations, you can keep your candidate flow at the same level and get your ratios down. That might mean that for every fifteen presentations you result in five interviews and one placement. 15: 5: 1. So for every thirty candidates you present, you close two deals a month. If your fees are $15,000 a month, two placements a month consistently gives you a $360,000 billing year.

To improve your ratios, you can only improve your skill level in the placement process. You do this by continually training and retraining, by role-playing, by journaling, and by being totally honest with yourself and your manager. You find out your areas of weakness and develop a game plan to improve those ratios. Ask yourself: "What areas of improvement in my desk would yield a better interview to placement ratio?" Ask yourself this question when journaling, and you'd be amazed at the answers your subconscious mind gives you through your written words!

After you've determined your interview to placement ratio from your past performance, you can now set a monthly goal for the number of interviews you must have to yield the placements, giving you your targeted revenue number. But don't focus on the revenue number. Focus on the interviews and the candidate presentations. If you know that for every five candidates you present, one gets interviewed, and if you need to set up twelve interviews that month, then you need to present sixty candidates. That's a lot of candidates for a search desk. It really depends, though, on how much candidate flow your office has. For a clerical and administrative desk, they actually might present five to ten candidates a day to clients.

But whatever your ratios turn out to be, you need to make the candidate presentations and the number of interviews be your primary focus. Forget about everything else: just focus on candidate presentations and interviews.

In addition to these two goals, presentations and interviews, you should also look at your yearly Life Goals and break each of them into monthly goals. Examples of this might include four dates with your spouse for family goals. Maybe you could read one fiction book for the month for your recreational goal. For family goals sometimes I've even included the goal of "only encouraging words" to make sure that I focus on positively communicating my love to my family. For mental goals, it might be taking a course or reading a training book on recruiting. But look at each category of your Life Goals, see where you want to go for your one-year goal, and write at least one or two goals for the month for each category. By working on each area of your life, you are maintaining balance and can have harmony between all areas.

And that's it for setting and tracking monthly goals. Usually I just put up tick marks on a dry erase board for each candidate presentation and each interview to keep track of it all. And at the end of the month, I document the number of presentations and interviews on an Excel spread sheet to maintain a library and history of my performance. That way I can graph out everything as well to see where any monthly deficits might have occurred.

Remember that what can be measured can be improved upon, and if we can physically see a long-term historical document on our performance, then we can get a good idea of what months usually result in bad production and can develop countermeasures to head off cyclical trends in our performance.

At the beginning of each week, I establish a goal for the number of presentations and interviews I am going to set up. In fact, before each and every day, I write down two or three major things that I want to accomplish that day to help me reach those weekly targets. It might be the number of candidates that I want to have positively respond to a recruit call. It might be the number of interviews that I set up, or the number of candidates that I present. Sometimes it might be just performance goals rather than production goals, goals that have to do with my performance rather than the end result. I might set a goal to just talk to forty people that day, or to dial the phone one hundred times that day. I don't care who says yes and who says no, just as long as I talk to forty people that day or reach my goal in the number of times I pick up the phone and dial it. Those performance goals tend to take the pressure off of me, knowing that if I just do what I'm supposed to, I'll have the results that I'm supposed to have. Shake up your daily goals. Make them interesting. See how long you can go before putting the handset back in the receiver. Just keep hitting your "flash" button on your phone. See how long you can go before you talk to anyone else in your office or how long you can go before you get up out of your chair. Make them fun and interesting. Have contests in the office. See who can sit in their chair the longest and make the first person that gets out of their chair buy bagels for everyone. (Just make sure they don't get a kidney infection from not going to the bathroom that morning.) Have fun with your daily goals.

I am always looking at my daily goals, my monthly goals, my yearly goals, and my five-year goals. I usually will tape my one and five year goals to the side of my computer monitor. For my daily goals, I will write them on my daily accountability sheet so that I can concentrate on them all day. Each day, I write down the two or three things that I want to accomplish in order to be successful at the end of the day. I focus on the vital factors that have to get done for me to consider the day a success.

Before you move on to the next chapter, review your five and one year goals. Make sure you have them written down for each of the categories that are important to you. Do you have them written down? Yes? If not put the book down NOW and write them down.

Do you have them written down? This ink is designed to smudge all over your hands if you don't. So don't you dare go further unless you've written down your five and one-year goal.

Are they done yet? Good. Let's keep going. Now, write those same categories down in your thirty-day format. Take each category and write down the two or three things that you would like to accomplish in the next thirty days.

Once you have your five-year, one year, and thirty day goals written down, cut them out and tape them to the side of your monitor at work. I know that's not very sexy and not very high tech. I know that what we should really do is create this complex computer program and keep the information on the server…right where you'll never see it again. So go ahead and use the monitor in the way that it was designed: a place to put yellow sticky notes and your goal sheets. Keep it right where you can see it all day.

Keep looking at your goal sheets throughout your workday. See yourself hitting each of your goals. Visually go into your mind's eye and see yourself hitting each of the goals. If one of your goals is a production goal, visualize yourself closing that last deal which puts you over the edge.

Whatever your goals are, see yourself reaching them and you'll be closer to actually doing so.

Chapter Ten

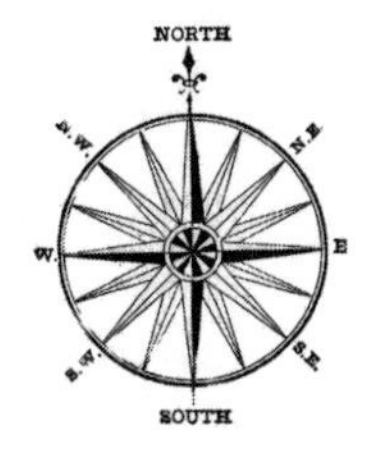

The Successful Failure

How to Keep from Being One

I heard a tape once on goal setting by Alec MacKenzie, the author of The Time Trap. The tape series was entitled "Managing Your Goals," produced by Nightingale Conant, and is one that I would recommend for any recruiter or manager that realizes that they are not reaching their fullest potential. In this series, the author tells a story about a goal-setting and performance improvement training session that he was doing for an insurance company. One of the top performers in that company was a young fellow in his late twenties who was doing exceptionally well compared to the rest of the representatives in the organization. He was earning a solid mid-six figure income, probably about $400,000 or $500,000 a year in income. After a few years, he became complacent with that performance and began to lose interest in the insurance industry. He was beginning to consider other career options up until the time that he spoke to the author about his performance. "I guess I seem to be losing interest in this. It seems to be happening, but I don't feel challenged." The author looked him in the eye and said that he was what was known as a successful failure.

A successful failure is someone who seems to be successful on the outside. They are earning a nice living and are a respected colleague among their peers. They are a top performer and seem to have a knack to make things happen. Things might even happen quite effortlessly for them, as it seemed to for this young insurance sales representative. To others, they seem successful. But the real issue is that of potential. What are you producing, and what is your potential of production? It is that difference, the "performance delta" between the two that can be a challenge for many recruiters. And it is that same difference, if not explored and developed, that can save the careers of many of those who become burned out in the business.

Are you a successful failure? Are you really doing everything it takes to reach your fullest potential in the staffing and recruiting industry? If there were no limits to your performance and you did your very, very best, what level of production do you think you could crank out in the course of a year? If you removed all distractions, if you took away all of the hindrances that stand in the way between you and your best year, what would your performance levels be? These are truly powerful questions and the answers can free you up to help you reach your best year.

Back before my wife and I had a baby, I used to love playing golf. (Now I just ponder in true amazement that I actually had an entire single four hour block of time to do anything fun that didn't involve changing diapers or chasing after an excited and happy little toddler. That in itself was unbelievable.) And I could have been a professional golfer. Yes, better than Tiger Woods or Jack Nicklaus. And I'm not exaggerating. I usually would play in the low 90's, but if it wasn't for my slicing I could have been on the tour. And the short game. If I had a better short game, I would be tour material. And the putting, too. My putting was okay, but that's because I didn't have the time to practice and I found it very boring. But if I had the time and the desire, I could out-putt Arnold Palmer on any day. Move over, Arnie. You've got competition! I can honestly say that if I didn't slice the ball, had a better short game, and could putt better, I would consistently be a better golfer.

But for ____________ (fill in the blank), I could reach my fullest potential as a recruiter. You get the picture.

There are certain issues, certain deficits that you have and display on your desk that are keeping you from reaching your fullest potential.

So, what are those deficits? What issues are preventing you from producing to the level that you've always wanted to achieve? In your personal success journal, write about these. Is it your selling skills? Your lack of organization? Your self-confidence? Your discipline? Is it a lack of knowledge about the business? Is it your knowledge of your industry niche? Is it too many client rejections? Too many candidate rejections? Are clients walking all over you and not returning your calls? Whatever it is, it's probably within your control. And if it's within your control, then you can have a direct impact on the outcome and your personal production. So right now, before you read any further, put the book down and grab a pen and begin journaling about those things that are keeping you from being more successful as a recruiter.

I've read about goal setting and the reward system. I've read and heard in seminars that you should set a goal and a reward mechanism that is somehow going to motivate you to achieve that goal. Personally, I find that method of thinking to be a short-term quick fix with less than optimal results. Rewards are fine, I suppose, but shouldn't be the driving force of a recruiter working a desk. Carrots only work for so long.

But then there's the stick. Ah, yes, the stick. The stick will keep my people moving. Yes, It will keep them moving all right...it'll keep them moving right through your doors to a competitor.

When people use rewards as incentives to reach goals they are going to give performance that is only meaningful at the superficial level. They will reach the goal, and finally upon reaching it, breath a sigh of exasperation and relief, being thankful that finally that whole ordeal is over.

When people are motivated by fear of punishment, you can count on them reaching their goals... once, maybe twice. But their hearts will not be in their work, and they will most likely be looking to relocate at the first possible opportunity.

What is more effective than this reward system, is the fundamental driving force of all major achievers. It is what keeps Bill Gates in the game, even though he's already won it. It is that desire to do your very, very best. Once you make the decision to operate at your maximum potential, even realizing that potential, then you will feel a surge of motivation run through you like electricity. Your motivation to get to work earlier will be there, and the desire to stay on the phone will increase. It is this desire to reach your fullest potential and to do your very, very best that will be your primary motivation, not that trip to the Bahamas that you've set if you hit your goals. Again, rewards are fun and can make your goal attainment interesting, and the stick can indeed, give you the results you are looking for, but neither are as effective as the sincere internal motivation that you can create to reach that fullest potential.

Chapter Eleven

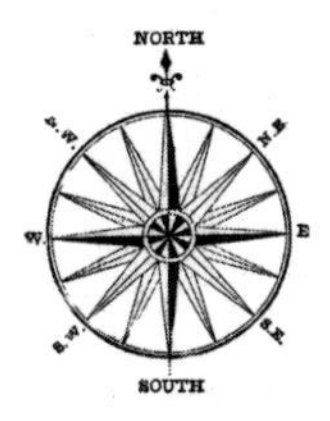

Maximizing Relationships

How to "Get the Call"

There is nothing more exciting in the world of recruiting than getting a message that goes something like this:

"My name is John Smith and I wanted to call you because I'm an attorney representing a company that is looking for a new president. I'd like to find out about your search capabilities and see if you'd be interested in helping us with this. Please call me at…."

That's a thrill. It's a rush. To know that your practice is actually on the map and that someone besides your mom actually visits your website.

Getting a call like that is a challenge, partly because you have no control over who is going to call you, and partly because it's like making gumbo soup: you never know how it's going to turn out regardless of what ingredients you put in to the equation. But there are certain principles that you can use that can guarantee this: **people will think of you first when they have a need.**

The concept of marketing was something that at one point I thought I knew nothing about. But the more I got involved in this business, the more I realized that I actually knew something on the subject. I've never really studied it before and I certainly haven't read too many books on marketing and branding. But I have learned this: the objective in effective marketing as a recruiter is to make sure that you are the first recruiter considered when a need comes up. That's it. That's how you know if your marketing campaign is successful. Focus on this singular objective and your marketing campaign will succeed. A marketing campaign isn't just something you do once. It's part of your daily habits as a recruiter.

Super-effective marketing is educating others around you that you are eminently more qualified than others who do what you do. If you can create the perception that you are more qualified than someone else, then you can capture the business. And it has nothing to do with price. It has everything to do with giving the perception of value, that the value for your service is greater than the cost. That the end result is worth the fee of hiring you.

So ask yourself: What is it that causes me to call on a certain professional service provider compared to someone else? Hmmm... let's see. I'd like to find the cheapest heart surgeon for my next transplant; or the cheapest accountant for my audit with the IRS. And I'd really like to find the cheapest lawyer to defend me at my next trial. That's the problem with many search professionals, they don't see themselves as professionals. They see themselves as a commodity because they've actually believed too many of their clients telling them that they're just a commodity. Come on. The reason those few clients told you that is because they want some sort of a little discount. They're not looking for huge discounts.

There's a profile of individuals out there who actually relish in saving a dollar a month on their office rent. They actually try to get free muffins from the bakery every once in a while. And a successful vacation includes a free upgrade to the concierge level of the hotel. They're not looking for you to give away your business or to drop your fees from 30% to 25%. They're just looking for some sort of preferred treatment, like a small discount. So give it to them. Give them the discount. "If you pay me within ten days of the candidate showing up, John, I'll give you a ninety day candidate guarantee free of charge. If you FedEx the check to me and I get it the day after he starts I'll throw in another two weeks of guarantee period for free." Be creative and give value to your clients that does not cost you a dime but gives them the perception of getting preferred treatment or some sort of a deal.

So what is it that causes you to call on a certain professional service provider first? The real reason is the fact that he or she is a certified bonafied guaranteed legitimate authority in their field. As a professional speaker, I market my speaking services to associations, companies, meeting planners, and speakers' bureaus around the country. In addition to targeting the recruiting industry, I also target corporate America and speak on the topics of leadership and employee retention. Who better to be a qualified expert on retention than someone who gets paid to "un-retain" employees? And in marketing myself, I have to show them without a doubt that I'm an authority on this subject. So I do this by including in my marketing materials publications that I've been quoted in, testimonials from other satisfied clients, credentials, and a summary of my career history. In the speaking business, it's paramount that a speaker show, to the end user, that he or she is not just qualified on the subject, but is an authority on it.

The fact that you're an executive recruiter gives the mystique to others that you hide behind this golden veil from the rest of corporate America, doing your magic and impressing everyone. If they only knew that we are just like the wizard from the Wizard of Oz. If they only knew that the recruiter is just a regular fellow or lady who gets frustrated with rejection and whose main career goal is to stay in the business until lunch. But we possess a mystique with the business, and just by being in the business we have credibility. People look at us like we have all the career answers and hold the "secret jobs" in our "secret job folder". So use it. Use this mystique to create some mystery about what you do.

In creating a marketing plan, ask yourself how you can come across to your clients, prospective clients and candidates as an authority in the field of recruiting. One way to gain immediate credibility is to gain a certification in the industry, known as the CPC (Certified Personnel Consultant). By doing this, you are showing your clients that you are a professional in the business, because many of them might choose to pursue the same level of excellence within their own respective industries. By doing this you are showing them that you, too, are a professional. If you want to deal with the higher-level authorities, you must start thinking like one. Research your clients' industry trade associations. See how many of them get involved in that association. Chances are that it's fairly common for your clients to do this, so if you follow their lead, they'll respect you. If they see some sort of certification after your name, your brand will be reinforced. You will be seen as an authority in the field of recruiting.

Remember that everything you do or say reinforces the continuity of your branding. If you come across as a rookie and sound like one and don't pursue any sort of industry legitimizing, then you will be perceived as less than professional. The concept of certification is indeed involved around knowledge learned which is tremendously valuable. I'm just looking at it from a branding and marketing standpoint. For more information contact the National Association of Personnel Services (NAPS) by visiting their website, www.napsweb.org. The requirements are at least two years in the industry and that you have to take the CPC test (for temp folks, it's another designation). The knowledge on the exam is relevant, useful, and interesting, and you will definitely use it someday. But as far as branding goes, you are separating yourself from the majority of the industry by choosing to get the designation. Does it have anything to do with bigger billings? Perhaps. That's more of an individual performance issue. This is just one way that you can contribute to your professional training, your branding, and serve your clients from more of a credible partner perspective than a recruiter perspective, which is what they want.

The press gives instant credibility. In a moment, your name is in print and the whole world knows that you are an expert on the recruiting industry. Are you going to get many calls from the article? Maybe one or two. But that article, if it's in printed media, can be used over and over again to leverage your credibility and to show your clients and prospective clients that you are unequivocally the ideal search partner for their search needs. In publicity, you don't pay for it and a journalist had to take the time to find out your thoughts on an issue and quote you as the expert. If it's in print then people will believe it.

Many years ago there was a tabloid paper that had a picture of former President Clinton shaking hands with an alien. Yes, an extra-terrestrial. It was in print, and I'm sure many people believed it. I also remember seeing that same tabloid talk about aliens landing on a U. S. Navy aircraft carrier. It even had a photo of an aircraft carrier with the flying saucer sitting on the flight deck parked next to several F-4 aircraft. The only problem with the photo, though, was that the F-4 had been phased out of use for many years prior to the photograph being allegedly taken. Hmmmm... But, it was in print, so I'm sure it happened.

There are several ways to go about getting good PR, and I've been down all these roads. The best way is to hire a public relations firm. This is also the most expensive. Perhaps you are promoting a new office that you're opening and want publicity in a new target market for a few months. Maybe you want to make a big push into a new sector that you're getting in to, such as high level retained work or executive contract staffing. Guard your wallet carefully and shop around if you're going to go this route. I did, and it proved very positive and gave me a lot of newspaper articles that I still use today in my marketing materials. But it was expensive.

Consider hiring an intern from your local university. Pay him or her a decent wage and find someone from the business school who wants to get into publicity. Hire a junior or a senior who has already had the important classes relevant to what you want them to do. That would be a great chance for a youngster to get some real-world experience with a real company, and to satisfy the requirements of their internship programs. Interns work very hard and are very sincere about what they do. And best of all, hardly any of them have ever heard of the Emancipation Proclamation so you can give them all the collateral duties that no one else wants to do.

Another route is to do it yourself. I'm sure you could take classes and read books on this subject, and that's fine if you have the time. I found a shortcut, though, and I want you to follow up on this if you're serious about getting your name out there. There is a publicity agent named Dan Janal who offers a service to business people. For a very small monthly or annual fee, you will receive bucket loads of requests from reporters looking for subject matter experts on a variety of topics. When you sign up for Dan's service, you can specify what topics that you would like to hear about. And at least three to five times a day, you will receive requests from reporters from major publications to smaller regional ones looking to quote some expert on a topic. You respond to the reporter via email, and if you're selected, you get quoted. And you can get a copy of that media and keep it forever. Show it to everyone. Your mom will be proud. Tell Dan you're a recruiter and that you read about his service in my book and he'll have an idea already about what topics would be best for you to receive in his daily emails. His website address is www.prleads.com.

Relationships are built with frequency of contact. Develop a system for getting back with people, specifically a quarterly call list. Each time I talk to a decision-maker, whether I'm checking a reference or marketing a candidate that he or she can't use right then, I send information out on my company and my personal background and also set them up in my computer system to put them on a quarterly call cycle. Sometimes I might not call them depending on how much I want to pursue the relationship, but at least I put my name in front of them five times a year. I use a software program that has been serving the staffing and recruiting industry for well over a decade, name Encore. Encore is developed by The Cluen Corporation out of New York, (www.cluen.com) and I am a strong advocate of their program. When I researched software programs, I diligently looked at about six or seven, and this one is the best. I stay organized and can automate my schedule, search for candidates, etc. The function I love the most, though, is having my key decision makers automatically receive correspondence from me. I write a newsletter, print it up, and have all the appropriate contact labels printed out from Cluen. I have my administrative assistant fold and send the mailings, and each quarter about 600 people get a newsletter and two business cards. It costs me money to do this, but the return on that investment ALWAYS occurs.

When writing a newsletter, divide it into two sections, and keep it to one page, front and back. Keep it in a three-column format and keep it short, sweet, and relevant. I've never read a newsletter from a sales representative promoting his or her services that was more than three or four pages; and have rarely made it to the third or fourth page. People are busy and you should respect that.

The first section of your newsletter should be a story about you. Don't write about why you're a great recruiter or your qualifications. Instead, tell a personal story about what you've done in the industry that others might find interesting. Or tell a story about your personal life that fits in with a concept in hiring or an issue in their industry. In a recent newsletter, I wrote about my toddler losing his "Construction Man" from his toy dump truck. I wrote about how we diligently searched the house and that he was so happy to have found his "Construction Man". Since I recruit in the commercial construction industry, I wrote a story about how fervent I was in my searching for my little boy's "Construction Man" the same way I fervently recruit for my clients. It was true, sincere, congruent, endearing, and I made money off of it. You can't lose when you just decide to be yourself, unless you're a freak or something like that. But most of us aren't. If you're in the staffing or recruiting business, then your coolness factor is definitely high. So be your own cool self and share who you are personally with your clients in your newsletter.

The second section of your newsletter should be focused on an issue that they are facing, and not necessarily about how you want to make placements in their organizations. Remember that your clients are sophisticated and they probably can sense if they're being manipulated on an issue. So find out what is a major challenge they are facing, and address that issue. If it's legitimately hiring related, write your article so that they can gain value even if they never call you. When you give away information that is not manipulated in your direction, you will get business from it. It's interesting how that works. When you're honest with people and can give them honest information that isn't manipulating them toward you, then they'll do business with you. The opposite holds true as well. If you are self serving and don't have your eyes focused on the interests of your clients, then they'll pick up on that as well and choose to do business with somebody else.

I physically send my newsletters out via US Mail. Snail mail. Takes five days to get there. And it gets read because they don't receive anything else like this in the mail; again, differentiation from competitors. Plus, I deliver two business cards to them each quarter. My name is in front of them all the time. So it costs me about $3.00 per year per contact including the cost of postage, business cards and envelopes. But the return is worth it. I always get calls that result in solid high-level search work. It might be a vice president who is looking to make a move and works with me exclusively to market him. Or it might be some solid search work from a client that has confidential replacement positions he's working on. Either way, it's worth it for me. This might or might not work for you depending on how well your relationship skills have been developed. If you're the kind of person who people remember and like, then this is going to work for you.

I've thought about sending out an email newsletter to my family of clients and candidates, but haven't done it yet and don't know if I will. There are so many email newsletters out there that one more just might end up getting deleted and I'm just not sure it would be effective for my niche. I do have a weekly Recruiter Tips newsletter that I send out to the recruiting industry for my speaking business through email in an html format, and that's helpful because most of the recruiters I target are looking for just one more tip that can help them become more successful.

(To register for this free service, visit my website, www.recrutingmastery.com. All you need to enter is your first name, email address, and zip code).

I suppose an email newsletter to clients and candidates might prove effective, but that would probably depend on your industry. With my mailing, I am sending something that they can physically keep and pass on to somebody else: a business card. Odds are that an email newsletter won't be memorialized as well as a tangible object that will sit in their desk drawer next to the Jolly Ranchers and paper clips that accumulate in their drawer organizers.

Each time I talk with a candidate or a client that I want to remember, and want to have remember me, they get a letter, two business cards, and a blurb on my own background within five days of my first contact with them. I want them to know that I'm an expert in their industry, so I include a few clients listed on my sheet. That's got to be one of the most effective tools in the business: giving everyone you talk to a brief bio on you and why you're qualified to recruit in their industry. Charles Wadlow from Seattle gave me that idea. The whole point of that letter, even though there's a cost, is that you will be remembered. These clients and candidates of ours get calls from unprofessional recruiters all the time. Because you're taking the time to improve yourself, I already know that you're a professional. So you can use this system to gain leverage over your competitors. After you talk with someone you want to keep in contact with, send them a letter telling them about your company, niches, and how you would like to help them when the time is right for them. I have one form letter I use for candidates and one for clients. Included in this is a sheet with my background and a list of some major clients that I've worked with. I even have a photo on the sheet because photos are powerful. People want to know whom they're developing the relationship with, so put your best mug shot on there and send it out. If you want copies of my form letters, call me at 1-800-930-3425 and I'll email them to you.

In addition to publicity, credibility, industry knowledge, and frequency of contact with people in your influence circle, a final and critical element of success in "getting the call" is your own personal relationship skills. Most of the people in this industry are very high on the coolness quotient. Most of us would rather play than work and that's why we do so well at this business: people tend to like being around people like us. We're upbeat. We're fun.

We're happy, damn it. Well, most of the time at least. But overall the majority of us have strong people skills.

If you don't have those skills yet, then you can develop them. And if you're not sure whether you have them or not, just look at how long you've been in the business and see how high your billings are. If they're not high, then you might want to consider working on you. You are your best investment and deserve the time and money that you should invest in yourself. In this business, your income increases when your personal growth increases. By learning and growing in your emotional intelligence, your income will increase. People will gravitate to you. You will be the one that people call on when they need help. Refer to the appendix for a listing of books that can help you grow in this area. And if you need to, write some personal growth goals in your personal success journal. Write down that you'd like to read two books this month on personal relationship skills.

A good rule of thumb regarding people is to remember two things: first, **people only do what is in their own best interests**, and second, that **people are consistent in their habits.** Basically that's all you need to know about people, and to treat them the way they want to be treated. Don't try to change or control people. People want to be led, not controlled. People will eagerly follow a leader who is "followable". If you grow in your own personal leadership, you will see your influence over people increase as well.

When I was nine years old, I lived in Japan for a short period of time and took Judo lessons from a Japanese master. The first thing we learned to do was to fall. The second thing we learned was not to fight your opponent. Instead, we learned to use your opponent's energy and leverage to your advantage. If your opponent comes running at you, use that running energy to trip or throw him to your side. If he swings at you, use his swing momentum to gain control over him.

In the same way, candidates and clients have their own agenda. They have their own best interests and that's just the way it's going to be. Instead of trying to change that agenda, find out what it is and go with it. Find out what type of ideal career scenario the candidate would love to hear about, and present your client's opportunity in that way. Find out what the ideal search firm looks like from a prospective client, and show him or her why your firm fits that description.

I heard an expression that states a common myth about masters of influence. You've probably heard it, too. You've heard a good salesperson as one who can "sell icemakers to Eskimos". That phrase carries with it some serious flaws about selling. Instead of pushing something to someone that they don't need, find out what they need and help them get that. Don't sell Eskimos icemakers. Sell them space heaters. You'll make more money that way. Find out what is important to your client and candidate and give that to them.

When people sense that you really do have their best interests at stake, then you'll be the first one remembered, the first one sought-after, the first one called.

Epilogue

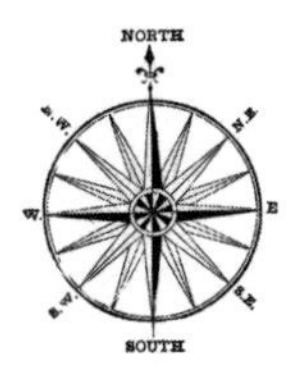

I have a strong level of attachment to someone who sits in my seminars or invests in my training materials. I care that you use this material to help you reach your goals, so if you have any suggestions, comments, questions, or ideas, please email them to me at scott@recruitingmastery.com. I also look for contributions to my email newsletter, *Weekly Recruiter Tips*, so if you have a good or a great idea, send me an email and I'll give you credit for it.

Always remember that this life that you've been given is not a dress rehearsal or a practice session. It's the real thing. This is the big game. Today is your chance of a lifetime, so stay strong, press on, seek out buried treasure, and keep your life filled with love, joy and adventure.

Now put this book down and get back on the phone.

Appendix

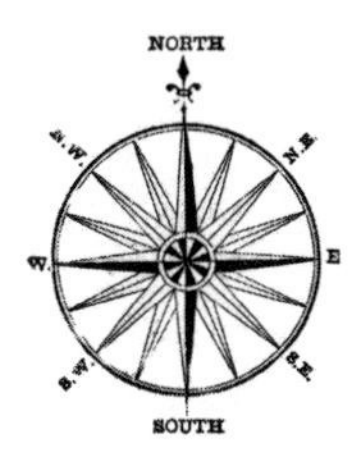

Adler, Lou. *Hire With Your Head.* New York, NY: John Wiley & Sons, Inc., 1998.

Alessandra, Tony, Ph.D. *Charisma: Seven Keys to Developing the Magnetism that Leads to Success.* New York, NY: Warner Books, Inc., 1997.

Bettger, Frank. *How I Raised Myself from Failure to Success in Selling.* New York, NY: Prentice Hall Press, 1947.

Cathcart, Jim. *Relationship Selling.* New York, NY: Pedigree Books, 1990.

Cialdini, Robert B., Ph.D. *Influence: The Psychology of Persuasion.* New York, NY: William Morrow & Company, Inc., 1984.

Cohen, Herb. *You Can Negotiate Anything.* Secaucus, NJ: Lyle Stuart Inc., 1980.

Collins, James C. and Porras, Jerry I. *Built to Last: Successful Habits of Visionary Companies.* New York, NY: HarperCollins Publishers, Inc., 1994.

Corson, Lynea, Ph.D, Hadley, George, Ed.D. and Steven, Carl, CPAE. *The Secrets of Super Selling.* New York, NY: The Berkley Publishing Group, 1991.

Covey, Stephen R. *The Seven Habits of Highly Effective People.* New York, NY: Simon & Schuster Inc., 1989.

Dawson, Roger. *Roger Dawson's Secrets of Power Negotiating.* Franklin Lakes, NJ: The Career Press, 1995.

Dolan, John Patrick. *Negotiate Like the Pros.* Brea, CA: LawTalk Publications, 2001.

Dornan, Jim and Maxwell, John C. *Becoming a Person of Influence.* Nashville, TN: Thomas Nelson, Inc., 1997.

Girard, Joe and Shook, Robert L. *How to Close Every Sale.* New York, NY: Warner Books, Inc., 1989.

Gitomer, Jeffrey H. *The Sales Bible.* New York, NY: William Morrow and Company, Inc., 1994

Hawkinson, Paul. *Closing on Objections.* St. Louis, MO: The Kimberly Corporation.

Hopkins, Tom. *How to Master the Art of Selling.* Scottsdale, AZ: Tom Hopkins International, Inc., 1980.

Hybels, Bill. *Who You Are (When No One's Looking).* Downers Grove, IL: InterVarsity Press, 1987.

Kaplan, Burton. *Winning People Over: 14 Days to Power and Confidence.* Englewood Cliffs, NJ: Prentice Hall, 1996.

Maltz, Maxwell., M.D., F.I.C.S. *Psycho-Cybernetics.* New York, NY: Prentice-Hall, Inc. 1960.

Mandino, Og. *The Greatest Success in the World.* New York, NY: Bantam Books, 1981.

Maxwell, John C. *The 21 Irrefutable Laws of Leadership.* Nashville, TN: Thomas Nelson, Inc. 1998.

Pitino, Rick and Reynolds, Bill. *Success is a Choice: Ten Steps to Overachieving in Business and Life.* New York, NY: Broadway Books, 1997.

Qubein, Nido R. *How to Get Anything You Want!* High Point, NC: Executive Press, 1998.

Rackham, Neil. *SPIN Selling.* New York, NY: McGraw Hill Book Company, 1988.

Robbins, Anthony. *Awaken the Giant Within.* New York, NY: Simon & Schuster Inc., 1991.

Robbins, Anthony. *Unlimited Power.* New York, NY: Ballantine Books, 1986.

Schiffman, Stephan. *Cold Calling Techniques (That Really Work!).* Holbrook, MA: Adams Media Corporation, 1987.

Schwartz, David J., Ph.D. *The Magic of Thinking Big.* New York, NY: Prentice-Hall, Inc., 1959.

Tracy, Brian. *Advanced Selling Strategies.* New York, NY: Simon & Schuster,Inc., 1995.

Waitley, Denis. *Empires of the Mind.* New York, NY: William Morrow and Company, Inc., 1995.

Ziglar, Zig. Top Performance: *How to Develop Excellence in Yourself & Others.* New York, NY: The Berkley Publishing Group, 1986.

Ziglar, Zig. *See You at the Top.* Gretna, LA: Pelican Publishing Company, Inc. 1975.